Courtesy PAC, Immigration Branch Records

"HARVEST EXCURSION. The Canadian Pacific Railway advise that the Harvest Excursion to the Northwest will be on August 31, 1904, from stations east of New Glasgow, and on September 1 from New Glasgow and stations west. Judging from the number of enquiries to date there will be a larger number from this section of the country.... It is hoped that the railway management will be better prepared for a large number this time than they were last year. It is also hoped that the weird tales from along the route of fighting, stealing, blood, and carnage will be lacking this year."

The Eastern Chronicle

Cape Bretoners "on the harvest" at Rathwell, Manitoba, 1914. Tom Smith, whose hand is on the steering wheel, and Milton Smith, sitting on the large wheel, were both from Smithville, Inverness County. Henry Smith, fourth from the right, was from Hillsborough, Inverness County. *(Courtesy Mabou Gaelic & Historical Society)*

THE
Harvest
Train

When Maritimers Worked
in the Canadian West
1890 - 1928

A. A. MacKenzie

with W. J. C. Cherwinski's
"The Incredible Harvest Excursion of 1908"

PHOTOGRAPHS

Breton Books

"The Incredible Harvest Excursion of 1908" by W. J. C. Cherwinski is printed from *Labour / Le Travailleur*, 5 (Spring 1980), with the permission of the publisher, the Canadian Committee on Labour History.

Selection from *I Came from Pictou County: Recollections of a Prairie Bluenose* is by Jane MacKay Rutherford, recorded and edited by Margaret Rutherford Davidson (Regina, 1976).

"The Old Harvest Train" by Vincent J. MacDonald, by permission of Claire MacDonald, first published in the *Sun*, Port Hawkesbury.

Selection from John Herd Thompson's "Bringing in the Sheaves: The Harvest Excursionists, 1890-1929," *Canadian Historical Review* 59:4 (1978), pp. 477-480.

"Steve Whitty: A Story and a Song," collected by Ronald Caplan, is from *Cape Breton's Magazine* Number 23, August 1979. The song was transcribed by Paul Stewart Cranford, www.cranfordpub.com.

Cover painting: Jan Wyers, "These Good Old Thrashing Days," with permission of MacKenzie Art Gallery, University of Regina Collection. Photographer: Don Hall. Copyright: Otto Wyers.

A. A. MacKenzie thanks Debbie Murphy and Juanita MacDonald, who typed the manuscript, and R. B. (Rae) Fleming, who edited it. For help with information on sources: Kathleen MacKenzie, Archivist, St. Francis Xavier University, Louis Hall, Jim Chapman, Murray Young, Doug and Mary Fraser, Gary Burrill, Duncan MacDonald, Bill Fraser of the RCMP, Dan and Effie Rankin, Mike MacMillan, Charles Walker, E. R. Forbes, R. J. Chisholm, Steve Cook, Allan Dunlop, Bill Copeland, Herb Dickeson, Ken Donovan, and Av Baldin. The publisher also thanks Gail Jones, Laura Syms, and Ken Donovan.

Book Editor & Designer: Ronald Caplan
Production Assistant: Bonnie Thompson

The Canada Council | Le Conseil des Arts
for the Arts | du Canada

We acknowledge the support of
the Canada Council for the Arts for our publishing program.

We also acknowledge support from Cultural Affairs,
Nova Scotia Department of Tourism and Culture.

NOVA SCOTIA

Tourism and Culture

National Library of Canada Cataloguing in Publication Data

MacKenzie, A. A. (Angus A.)
    The harvest train : when Maritimers worked in the Canadian West, 1890-1928
Including "The incredible harvest excursion of 1908," by W. J. C. Cherwinski.
Includes bibliographical references.
ISBN 1-895415-64-0

    1. Maritimers—History. 2. Prairie Provinces—History. I. Cherwinski, W. J. C. (Walter Joseph Carl), 1942- Incredible harvest excursion of 1908. II. Title.

HD1530.P76M33 2002   362.82'92'09713   C2002-900389-X

CONTENTS

PHOTOGRAPHS

CHAPTER 1

Some Wild and Woolly Times

IN AUGUST 1909 the *Edmonton Bulletin* noted that "the harvester excursions are running. It is the time for the people of Northern Ontario to take to the woods."[1]

Harsh words, but only a slight exaggeration. The harvest excursions were a great and unique national enterprise. They brought thousands of people from the eastern provinces and British Columbia into the Prairies to harvest the grain crop—wheat, oats, and barley. Trains carrying harvest workers from the Pacific coast or the central provinces seem to have had quiet trips. But some of the Maritimers literally raised hell on their long journey that began in Sydney, Halifax, or Saint John.

In 1907 a farmer in Indian Head, Saskatchewan, clearly thought little of the "Down Easters," though he hired them to pick stones and kept them around until his crop ripened. "Nova Scotians are miserable toughs and worse," he told Colchester and Hants County men, "but I never saw one that wouldn't work."[2]

A seventeen-year-old man from Blandford, Nova Scotia, witnessed the sort of activity that gave Maritimers a hard name:

"On August 13, 1924, we paid twenty-six dollars for a return ticket from Chester to Winnipeg.... The men on these excursions were from all walks of life, and I can assure you that some of them were shady characters.... When we were compelled to stop for various reasons such as taking on water or a breakdown, all hell broke loose. Haystacks were set on fire, cars were overturned and things were stolen from stores. The train that went ahead of us by about three hours with the so-called harvesters had caused so much damage in one particular place that as our train sped through the night the villagers were so instilled with rage that they threw rocks through the windows for revenge. I came near to losing my life in that one.... After spending two months in the west I returned home, not rich but having obtained some knowledgeable experience."

He lost all his savings to a con man in Montreal![3]

An Annapolis Valley man who stayed in the West to study and practice medicine witnessed similar scenes on his week-long journey in 1898.[4]

NOW ALL THESE ACCOUNTS might be dismissed as exaggerations from old men looking back through the mist of years. But a reputable academic, Dr. Walter Cherwinski, has examined newspaper accounts concerning the six trainloads of Maritimers who headed west in August 1908. That excursion seemed marked by misfortune right from the beginning: a young farmer from Prince Edward Island was killed jumping from the train at Kensington. At Chalk River, Ontario, two days out, there was a minor train wreck that delayed the leading trainload of Maritimers for an hour. The five hundred or so excursionists were tired, bored, and thirsty. The men left the train and descended on the local hotel. They threw out the owner who tried to resist them, carrying off over a thousand dollars' worth of liquor and cigars, and the cash register containing three hundred dollars, along with the water tanks in each car which they had filled with draft beer.

Fights broke out as booze took effect. The lone Canadian Pacific Railway [CPR] constable was ignored as men ranged throughout the trains. Other trains had reached the site and stopped. The revellers tried to lynch one excursionist but he was rescued by his friends.

Each stop after the wreck site was cleared brought more excitement. Merchants in each town locked their premises, but excursionists broke down the doors and took what they wanted. At Mackey's Station they raided the station agent's home and demolished the furniture. In another community they reportedly drank three taverns dry in a few minutes. Farther on, the men raided a garden tended by two sisters and when the women protested, the hungry raiders pelted them with onions. At another station an insulted woman shot at the train, wounding a man from Merigomish, Nova Scotia. A specially reinforced North Bay police contingent, forewarned by telegram, met the first train. They arrested seven men for "attempted hooliganism" but let them get back on the train when it was ready to leave.

Back on the train the "drink-crazed brutes" continued the rampage. Some produced firearms, shooting at an Indian sitting on an embankment. She escaped, but a horse at another place was not so lucky. Bottles were thrown at section men working on the track, causing several to be hospitalized. On board, the train windows and lights were smashed and the cars left in "a disgraceful condition." A few women on one train were herded into a single car where several were raped. One Maritime schoolteacher allegedly was stripped and assaulted several times.

The train reached Fort William on August 14. There Lewis Cuttle, a one-armed, fifty-year-old harvester from Truro, was arrested for having Chalk River liquor on him, and another man was led away for breaking a glass door on the train. Cuttle was released—the booze theft had not occurred on CPR property. Another man pleaded drunkenness while smashing up railroad property. He was fined twenty dollars and damages. Two Nova Scotians received nine-month jail terms for breaking telegraph insulators. They pleaded drunkenness but a railway policeman said they were sober at the time. Presumably they smashed the insulators by throwing stones at them and were sober enough to have good aim!

West of the Lakehead—beyond Lake Superior— the Maritimers on the first train let fly a bombardment of bottles, cans, and other missiles at Doukhobor and Italian labourers employed at doubling the main CPR line. The later trains coming through at night were subjected to a hail of missiles from the enraged workers. Two harvesters were injured, others sought refuge from the fusillade in the upper berths. Revolvers were used to "defend the train" from the foreigners. Two Italian rail workers near Kenora were wounded by bullets. Another was killed by a heavy bottle thrown from the train. A disreputable lot of harvesters ended their four-and-a-half-day ordeal at the CPR depot in Winnipeg.[5]

Even after their ordeal, many harvesters could not get work on the farms. In many places that year the crop had short straw, requiring less effort and fewer workers. Far more harvesters had come out than were required. Many had to take railroad construction jobs or other work to earn the eighteen dollars for fare back home. Others were fed and sheltered by the Salvation Army.[6]

PROFESSOR CHERWINSKI in his account of the 1908 fiasco suggests that it was not typical of all excursions. Weather, bad planning, and unemployment in eastern centres had combined to cause a surplus of workers to be taken out, including many unemployed city workers who were lost on western farms. As for the violent behaviour of Maritimers, it was not a novelty—they had raided stores in Ignace in 1906, stealing all the bottled liquor in the stores and filling the train water coolers with draft beer. Winnipeg police, being apprised of this behaviour by telegraph, had arrested the first men off the train. Their mates piled off the cars through the broken windows, cut the traces on the paddy wagons and freed their mates. Police were helpless.[7]

It is clear that the lack of law enforcement on trains and at stations was an important factor in the spread of violence. Railway police had no jurisdiction off railway property. Local police were only interested in getting the "invaders" out of town. The Royal North West Mounted, except in exceptional circumstances, had no jurisdiction outside the Northwest—the territories and provinces between Ontario and the Rockies. After the Royal Canadian Mounted Police [RCMP] came into being in 1920, many of their officers rode the trains, bringing about a decrease in looting and violence. In fact a railway official declared in 1921 that because of the Mountie presence "for the first time rowdyism did not predominate on these trains all the way from the Maritime Provinces to Western Canada."[8]

This is not quite true—the excursion trains that

followed the "wild" earlier trains in 1908 were policed by special constables hired by the railways to prevent a repetition of the affair. The 2500 harvesters that arrived in Winnipeg on August 22, 1908, were quiet and respectable.[9] For that matter, the interviews recorded in this book show that many trains were orderly and peaceful. Others were not. In 1928, the last year that harvest trains ran from Maritime stations, Seldon Higgins of Lindsay Lake boarded the Cape Breton train in Truro. He witnessed no fighting on the train, though there was some looting at stops. Five Mounties boarded the train at a stop in the province of Quebec and took men off.

In 1926 the Deputy Minister of Labour sent the RCMP Commissioner a clipping from the *Ottawa Journal* detailing harvester outrages in that year. He mentioned Cochrane station. It is on the CNR route, the old National Transcontinental Railway. And, for some reason, while the CPR continued to ask for Mounties to maintain order on harvest trains throughout the period 1921 to 1928, the CNR did so only for the period 1921 to 1923, at least as a regular practice. The Deputy Minister wrote:

"Harvesters bound from Nova Scotia to the western wheat fields wrecked the Empress Hotel in Cochrane today. The proprietor objected to being bullied by them when the train was stopped. The Railway Police stood by and watched; local constables arrived too late. There have been reports of people being killed by bullets from these trains in other years, of women and children being dragged aboard the trains, outraged and cast out."[10]

CHAPTER 2

Why Were Maritimers Wanted in the West?

WHY WAS IT CONSIDERED NECESSARY to bring workers to the Prairies for the harvest?

Part of the answer was connected with the state of farm mechanization at the time. It was possible for a farmer on 160 acres—a quarter section—to plant his crop with horse-drawn disc seed-drill, having only his family and a hired man to assist him; but to cut and stook the ripened crop required one or two extra workers. After the grain ripened in the stook a certain length of time, a whole crew of workers was needed to haul the loads of sheaves to the separator—threshing machine—and transport the threshed grain to granary or elevator. More help might be needed in the house to feed the extra workers.

On the Canadian prairies, unlike in the United States, no large industrial centres existed to provide a pool of casual labour for the harvest, or to provide jobs for the extra harvesters; and there were no well-paid opportunities for farm employment in the winter.[1] The workers who would be needed part of the year could not be found locally. Before tractors came into common use—and that took place in the 1920s—several teams of horses were needed on every farm to pull the implements.[2] Farmers also grew much of their own food—poultry, livestock, and vegetables. The farmer's family and one hired man were enough to care for the livestock in the winter. Extra hands were needed only during the frenzied activity of August and September.

Wheat was the main cash crop. The development of dry-land farming techniques and of new wheat varieties extended the wheat-growing area. The expansion of railroad facilities that occurred with the boom in branch line construction enabled farmers to get their grain to market. The Canadian Pacific, Canadian Northern, and Grand Trunk Pacific engaged in a frantic race to build branch lines. The railroads "added 4,161 miles to their systems...from 1923 to 1931. Canadian Pacific branches totalled 2,266 miles, those of the Canadian National 1,895 miles.... Almost half of the $138 million spent by the two companies represented lines in Saskatchewan, and expenditures on the prairies as a whole exceeded $106 million— over three quarters of the total."[3] This superb transportation network allowed thousands of workers to be distributed throughout the region wherever they were most needed.

The railroad companies were vitally interested in the grain harvest, as a very large part of their traffic was in the carriage of grain to ocean ports and to the Lakehead; the railways had a heavy investment in grain elevators at the ports. Through its elevators and over its lines the CPR alone moved over 395 million bushels of wheat in the bumper crop year of 1928, over 100 million more than in a single season before.[4]

But the harvest excursions actually began as an extension of the CPR practice of running low-cost "Homeseeker Excursions" to people expressing an intention to buy railway lands. In response to requests from the government of Manitoba, in 1890 the CPR made empty seats on these excursion trains available to farm workers. By 1896 the railway was advertising excursions to be made up entirely of harvesters. The system was copied by the Soo line, the Canadian Northern, the Grand Trunk Pacific, the Intercolonial, and eventually by the CNR.

In early August, harvesters could buy a low-priced ticket on a special train heading west. Occasionally, a harvesters' car might be attached to a regular express, but usually the train was devoted to harvesters. The cost was generally half that of the regular fare. After thirty days' work at the harvest, attested to by a farmer or farmers who signed a ticket stub or similar document declaring that the harvester had worked, he could buy a ticket back home at slightly more than, equal to, or even less than, the fare out.[5]

To control the influx of workers, sometime after the 1908 "incredible mess" the terminus of all harvest excursion tickets was fixed at Winnipeg. Special booths were set out on the station platform—no letting those "savages" into the sacred confines of the station. The tariff from Winnipeg to any station on the prairies was one half cent a mile. Veteran harvesters warned newcomers to check the mileage to their destination: it was not uncommon for ticket sellers to add extra mileage, putting the overcharge in their pockets.

Sometimes the return fare was slightly higher—a mild incentive for harvesters to remain in the West, to become settlers. That was a secondary reason for setting up the harvest excursion: it would help to settle the West. The railroad companies, after all, had millions of acres of land for sale. Harvesters might elect to buy some of that land in the Fertile Belt instead of buying cheaper government land. Even if they chose to live in urban areas, they would swell the ranks of available workers and so help to keep wages down. Of the 10,004 harvesters making the journey in 1899, one third went out with the intention of settling. By 1905, according to the Department of Agriculture and Immigration, more than one half of the 13,000 harvesters elected to remain in the prairie country.[6]

These are estimates, likely optimistic estimates, by bureaucrats anxious to justify their existence. John Herd Thompson throws cold water on them:

"One of the enduring myths about the harvest excursions is that they provided a medium through which an Easterner could come west, earn a stake, and establish himself as a successful farmer.... Men who became even moderately wealthy, however, usually worked outside agriculture, and simply used the harvest excursion rates to obtain a low one-way fare."[7]

A good example is that of two brothers from Sunny Brae, Pictou County, who went out on the 1904 excursion. They became skilled in sheet metal work in Winnipeg and began manufacturing airplane floats. By 1948 the business created by Jim and R. F. Grant MacDonald employed 450 workers. Along with seaplane floats for a world-wide market they made farm implements and electronic gear.[8]

W. A. Bigelow from Kingsport, Nova Scotia, became a medical doctor, as did W. O. Chestnutt from Sussex, New Brunswick.

Everett Taylor from Prince Edward Island became a railroader. So did Duncan Fraser of MacLellan's Brook, and many others. Edward Campbell of East Lake Ainslie taught school in Saskatchewan. Many Nova Scotians—like Maurice "Blue" MacDonald, Murdock Sampson, and Gus MacNeil—worked in the western coal mines. And a host of people like

Lorne Robson of North Sydney went to the United States.

A young teacher from West River Station, Pictou County, Marjorie MacKenzie, took the excursion train in 1913. She was met in Winnipeg by her cousin Daniel MacKenzie, a sergeant on the police force there. He found accommodations for her and three other girls in the YWCA. Marjorie "got a school" near Vermilion, Alberta, through a Regina agency run by a Miss Nelson from Shubenacadie. Isabel McLeod, one of Marjorie's travelling companions, got a job in a jewelry store owned and operated by a Halifax man.[9]

Maritimers found other Maritimers everywhere in the West, but only a few of them were farming. And many of them had gone out on settlers' excursions. Reverend George Roddick led a number of Pictou County people to the Brandon Hills even before the CPR went through—they travelled on American lines. For example, Jack Cunningham in the 1920s homesteaded in the Carrot River Valley of northern Saskatchewan near a settlement of Nova Scotians who went out earlier.

The majority of Maritimers who took up homesteads did so before 1914 when land was comparatively cheap. CPR land was priced at $5.00 an acre in 1906, $11.00 in 1910, $21.53 by 1917.[10]

Even with the increase in wages that occurred through those same years, it was impossible for harvesters to scrape up enough for a down payment on the shrinking amount of good farm land available. The cost of getting a farm up and running exceeded what one could earn at the seasonal harvest:

"As George Edwards told a conference discussing the failure of the 1928 excursion from Britain, there was 'no hope' that these men 'would be able to take up farms for themselves, as they could not save enough from their earnings to keep themselves in clothing.' Because of the near-impossibility of becoming established as western farmers, virtually all of the British miners eventually returned home, and throughout the 1920s about 80 per cent of those who came to the Prairie provinces from Eastern Canada used their return coupons to go home at the conclusion of the harvest."[11]

"In addition to wages, however, there was the dream of independence and a farm of one's own, particularly powerful in the years before 1914, when accessible homesteads were still available. The dream of independence was nurtured by conditions at home, where, as one harvest excursionist recalls, farmers' sons 'were little more than slaves or chattels' receiving nothing more for their toil than the promise of an eventual inheritance. To such boys 'going West was a chance for freedom...and the cost was incredibly small.'"[12]

JUST IN PASSING, it seems distinctly unfair that the homestead system—160 acres of "free land"—was not available for "bachelor women." Only homesteaders' widows could take advantage of the Homestead Act. The Act enabled a family to acquire 160 acres almost free of charge, with the right until 1918 to "preempt"—that is, to eventually take over an adjoining 60 acres. Any unmarried woman with the courage to defy the conventions of the day and try to "make a go" of farming on her own had to actually buy the land. It was only after a long struggle that Alberta women, in 1930, were able to take advantage of the homestead system. The other two Prairie provinces did away at that time with homestead rights entirely.[13] Just in time for the Depression!

CHAPTER 3

Aboard the Trains

QUESTIONING A MAN in his nineties, still quite
alert and active:

Q. Why did you go on the harvest, Mr. Polson?

A. Well, for adventure. It was a good chance to see
the country!

Q. And make some money?

A. Hell, no! They would only pay two dollars a day
and board. You could get that in Antigonish County in
1903.

Q. Were there any wild times on the train?

A. No, it was quiet that year. But in 1905 there
was a bunch of toughs on—foreigners from the steel
plant in Sydney—they were building it then. Somewhere in Ontario they got mad about something that
happened at a station. When they got back on they
smashed all them damn wooden seats into splinters.
We had to sleep on the floor the rest of the way!

WELL, YOU MIGHT SAY that the "colonist cars"—
the rail cars on which they travelled—left an indelible
mark on the harvesters' minds as well as on their bod-
ies. One of the printable descriptions of the colonist
car was in *The Toronto Star*:

"The majority have slat seats, the kind that leave
marks. A few have thin cushions. At night the slat
seats are pulled out and beds formed in the same way

as the ordinary Pullman. But they are not Pullman beds. The passengers carry their own bed linen in the form of quilts and blankets and there is no porter to tuck them under their chins at night."[1]

Louis Hall, Taymouth, New Brunswick, recalled his gruelling trip:

"I was a little guy. It was bad enough sittin' on them hard-arsed seats all day in a car with no springs. I had to share that wooden shelf overhead at night with another skinny young feller. I tell you we were well acquainted by morning!

"They say the CPR changed from wooden coaches to steel ones because trains sometimes had to stop to pick up harvesters who had shot out of an upper bunk on those whiplash curves along Lake Superior. They'd go right through the opposite side of the car and out onto the right-of-way!

"Never killed any of 'em though: you had to be tough to go on the harvest."

On that car in 1926 were two old men going out as teamsters. One of them woke Louis and everyone else with bullroars of "Whoa! Whoa! You son of a bitch!" He was tuning up his vocal cords for the half-broken horses on prairie farms.

The colonist cars—called "immigrant cars" in the United States—were third-class passenger coaches used to take immigrants to the western prairies. They held fifty-six to seventy-two passengers, and contained a stove or two and a water cooler. They were built to last—some of them outlived most of the harvesters. They became armed forces' sleepers on troop trains during the Hitler war. A few were in branch line service until the 1960s. A car built by Silliker's in Halifax was given to the National Museum of Science and Technology in 1967. One car off the Canadian

Northern was still listed by the CNR as "in service" in 1992.[2]

Many a harvester wished the colonist cars were elsewhere, in a warmer climate, by the time he reached Winnipeg. There the excursionists were met by employment agents and farmers' agents outside the station, trying to lure them to different areas. Most Maritimers ignored them, bought their tickets, and headed for places they had worked before or where the "moccasin telegraph" rumour said the crop was heavy.[3]

AFTER THE 1908 FIASCO the Dominion government, western governments, and railroads had co-ordinated their efforts. Putting together reports from station agents, farmers, railway officials, farmer organizations, and others, the provincial and federal governments would strike a figure as to the number of harvesters required. In 1928 they estimated that 75,000 would be needed across the Prairies. Twenty-five thousand were thought to be available locally. Six thousand might be available in British Columbia. This left 44,000 to be brought from Eastern Canada or elsewhere.

The table on the following page shows the number of harvesters brought into the Prairie provinces from 1920 to 1930.

It is not possible to state the number of harvesters from just the Maritimes for any year but 1901. In that year 15,778 harvesters came from Ontario and Quebec, and 2,597 from Maritime points—roughly 14% of the total.[4]

Harvesters often came up from the United States on the Soo or Great Northern. Four hundred came across the International Border in 1905, one thousand in 1909, one thousand in 1910. These people apparently paid the full rate.[5] British workers were always present in small numbers. Many who came in 1927

THE ORIGIN OF HARVESTERS 1920-1930				
YEAR	EASTERN CANADA	BRITISH COLUMBIA	BRITISH ISLES	TOTALS
1920	28,228			28,228
1921	28,029	4,397		32,426
1922	35,570	4,170		39,740
1923	34,599	4,019	11,833	50,451
1924	21,131	5,351		26,482
1925	45,379	9,471		54,850
1926	24,662	7,336		31,998
1927	24,547	7,703		32,250
1928	34,158	9,737	8,330	52,225
1929	3,519			3,519
1930	13			13

and 1928 became the subjects of international controversy, discussed in Chapter 7.

The use of Japanese labour from the Pacific Coast was suggested in 1902 but firmly rejected; the use of Orientals would not be countenanced "until every other resource has been exhausted."[6] The colour bar was not strictly observed: A number of harvesters speak of "jolly musical dancing black men"—a common stereotype—on harvest trains from the Maritimes. However, six black men from Barbados who were apparently on a CPR harvest train in 1908 were jailed for vagrancy in Estevan.[7] There were even gradations of worthiness among "whites" who might settle in the West. La Touche Tupper, an "agent of the Manitoba government," visited Nova Scotia in 1901 encouraging harvesters to make the journey with a view to settlement. He warned them that the Prairies were in danger of being swamped by "American land-grabbers" and by "members of the Latin race."[8]

REGIONALISM, NOT ETHNICITY, was one of the factors in the frequent violence on harvest trains. For Maritimers it was nothing new. The "Judique Flyer"—the train from the Strait of Canso to Inverness—was the scene of many wild brawls, especially on weekends, among drunken Cape Bretoners. Colin MacFarlane, a telegrapher who often used the Flyer, told a story about teeth that would be flying in the coaches like cracked corn to the hens, while blood splashes were everywhere.

The Miramichi "Dungarvon Whooper" and other trains carrying New Brunswick lumberjacks had their share of brawls. A trainman in those times, like a small-town cop, had to be able to fight.

On the excursion train, however, diplomacy was better than fisticuffs—trainmen were heavily out-numbered. There developed a spirit of unity among the harvesters in any one car—"We fought among ourselves until we hit the mainland," said a Cape Breton man, "then we stuck together like glue."

Hundreds of miners and steelworkers took the train, especially during the hard times of industrial shutdowns and long strikes that marred the 1920s in Nova Scotia.

In 1923, a Glace Bay man boarded a train with many young unemployed miners. Men from Caledonia gathered in one coach, New Aberdeen men in another, christening their respective coaches Caledonia Local and Phalen Local after the two local branches of the United Mine Workers. Dan Brodie, elected president of the Phalen Local for the trip, had a quiet time of it:

"There were over five hundred harvesters on the train, one coach being reserved for women and men with their wives, some of whom went as cooks and helpers.... Ours was a CNR train.... Shortly after leaving Cape Breton everyone put away his best clothes and donned his khaki overalls. Everyone had his war bag and grip with blanket and overcoat. Most of us took our grub along with us and a mug for coffee.

"How did we pass the time? Well, getting up in the morning, stowing away our gear, and making ready three meals which we did in groups, getting ready for the bunk again at night.... Between times we raided coaches or stood off a good-natured raid from them. One bald head...had a face painted on it in shoe blacking while its owner slept. We got together in groups and sang in English and Gaelic to the accompaniment of mouth organs or just plain train rattle.

"The CNR policemen aboard [Thomas and Mac-Aulay] accompanied harvesters from Sydney right to Quebec province. The CNR police used to come in and join in the Gaelic singing. They were two splendid fellows and put us wise to all the tricks of making things comfortable on the trip.

"We ate, slept, danced when possible, told stories, swapped books, bragged of the accomplishments of ourselves (and relatives). When the cops turned us over to the Mounties and Quebec train police, I overheard the Frenchmen ask anxiously, 'What kind of crowd you got, eh?' 'Best crowd that ever came west,' said MacAulay.... The boys turned out in force and gave Thomas and MacAulay a big farewell.... My, weren't the French cops nice to us after that! They would get off at the station and help serve us in the stores and see that everyone got fair play.

"A lot of the trouble with harvesters has been the

fault of some greedy trader asking exorbitant prices."[9]

On the 1928 harvest Dan Allan Gillis witnessed a stirring scene when a courageous young policeman in one town got the crowd's attention, and pleaded with them to spare the town: "They're good people here, working people, they've been good to me." The Cape Bretoners carried him on their shoulders, would have killed anybody who damaged anything in that town!

The hiking of prices at stops to take advantage of the captive clientele on the excursion trains was a common cause of trouble. In 1921 the Palliser Hotel at Smith's Falls raised the price of beer to an exorbitant level. Harvesters complained and the local police chief persuaded the hotel manager to lower the price. At Chapleau the price of bread and sandwiches had been hiked upwards in the CPR restaurant, causing harvesters to boycott it.[10]

In 1923 the Mounties acted as escorts on twenty-seven CP and twenty-seven CN excursion trains from Eastern Canada with about 25,000 passengers. Two policemen were on each train. They restrained a lunatic and seized a few pistols, but pronounced most harvesters quiet and orderly, though excessive prices along the line caused ill feeling. Prices were exorbitant for the time: twenty-five cents for a sandwich and cup of tea, ninety cents for a pie, twenty-five cents for a quart of milk.[11]

Commissioner C. W. Harvison of the RCMP rode the harvest trains both as passenger and as escort. In 1919 he went west to work on the harvest and on his uncle's farm until he would be old enough to join the Mounted Police. Boarding the excursion train in Ontario, he judged the passengers to be respectable citizens—labourers, craftsmen, skilled workers—all bent on making a stake against what promised to be a rough winter. The postwar depression had set in and times were bad.

Young Harvison wondered initially how the harvesters had gained a riotous reputation. He soon found out. In most towns the merchants charged prices only a little higher than normal. But in a few places the prices were little short of robbery: One dollar for a loaf of bread or a bottle of milk or a pack of cigarettes. Most harvesters were short of funds. Small wonder, said Harvison, that there were fights and near riots.

After the harvest he joined the Royal North West Mounted in Regina, conveniently adding a year to his age on the application form, since he was not old enough to join—and no birth certificate was required.[12]

In August of 1922 the young constable boarded a harvest train in eastern Quebec as one of the escorting officers. Four Mounties were on each train.

"The train on which I was to travel originated in Nova Scotia and carried about seven hundred passengers.... We went through the train chatting with passengers and inquiring as to the cause of the troubles—some of them of riot proportions—that had erupted in some of the stopping points the previous year."

The Mounties explained their game plan to the harvesters, asking them to stay on the station platform until the police gave them a signal. They would talk to merchants, telling them that they would stay to maintain order as long as reasonable prices were charged. If prices were outrageous the cops would return to their trains and let the harvesters take over. The latter were asked to report excessive prices to the police. This ploy worked well until a storekeeper in Northern Ontario, aware that harvesters were short of supplies—at the previous stop all stores were closed and boarded up—put prices up several times above normal.

Things got ugly. The merchant, who had the only store in town, maintained that he had a right to charge whatever prices he wished. Some rocks began to fly. But the train crew was alert. The engineer whistled off and started the coaches moving. Passengers raced to get aboard. The train stopped within a few hundred yards, while the Mounties talked turkey to the merchant who feared that he might be left with the extra supplies he had stocked in hopes of gouging the harvesters. He brought down his prices, the train was backed up to the station, and the harvesters stocked up at fair prices. This pattern was repeated with other trains. No trouble that year, said Harvison.[13]

THINGS HAD CHANGED FOR THE BETTER since 1908. It was around that time that a little boy who later became a well-known Halifax journalist saw the harvest special pull out of the old North Station with everybody drunk aboard her, including the train crew. The engineer had to be carried aboard.[14]

In 1920 a New Glasgow town policeman returning from the harvest excursion told the *Eastern Chronicle* of seven hundred harvesters leaving a trail of destruction wherever the train stopped. Stores were looted, stations reduced to rubble. Carloads of sheep were let loose in one station; a shoe store was looted by raiders who sold them to others on the train for a couple of dollars. The buyers threw them out the windows when they heard that they might be arrested in Winnipeg if the shoes were in their possession. A Collie man lost his leg on the train while George Matheson, sixteen years old, was shot and killed at Cochrane.[15]

Editor James A. Fraser found the seeds of misbehaviour in the Tory government:

"The disgraceful behaviour of harvesters beating up people in Quebec was the harvest from seed sown by the Union Government in 1917. Railway police on the train were helpless, town police were threatened at stations. A man trying to protect his property with a gun was disarmed and chased into the woods. We are told," trumpeted James A. Fraser, "that last year a schoolteacher was plucked from the schoolhouse step, stripped naked and left on top of a freight car. The harvesters behaved as badly as German soldiers in Belgium—the trains should be followed by a regiment of armed soldiers hereafter."[16]

AN OLD SOLDIER who took the excursion train out of Saint John in 1920 saw little violence. Frank Parker Day was not a normal sort of harvester: large, burly, and well-dressed, he had an air of authority. Not at all surprising: he had been a Rhodes Scholar, a heavyweight boxing champion, commanding officer of a Nova Scotian Highland regiment, and author of the novel *Rockbound*. On the train he felt conspicuous, discovered that he was suspected of being a CPR detective, and let himself go—neglecting to wash or shave. The car was soon filthy—the crew made no attempt to keep it clean. Day got a broom at a stop and organized a clean-up gang on his car, sweeping three times a day. Other cars were like pigpens—the floors awash with tobacco spit. Day persuaded his personnel to spit out the windows. On that car food was picked up after each meal, the dish cloths were washed and hung out the windows. Hymns were sung on Sunday.[17]

Tranquillity vanished at station stops, however. Day witnessed harvesters living up to their rowdy reputation. They fought with local people about hens they tried to steal—rocks on one side, sticks on the other. At Schreiber, Ontario, many from the train were already out of food. At a grocery store there, clerks would hold firmly onto food with one hand until they got money in the other. Winchester rifles lay in easy reach of the clerks; a policeman threatened the crowd with a revolver. Fences were torn up for firewood, insulators broken on the telegraph line, cows were chased or milked in fields. Trees were pulled up and stuck all over the cars so the train looked like Shakespeare's Birnam Wood.

Day saw the harvesters as possessed by a compulsion to defy authority, to smash and destroy things. He compared the trip, with its discomfort, noise, and violence, to Robert Louis Stevenson's trip across the American Great Plains in the 1870s. But the comparison is seriously flawed. R.L.S. encountered dirt, bad manners, sickness, and uncouth behaviour when he traversed the plains on the emigrant cars of the Union Pacific, but no actual violence.

It is worth noting that Day, like the great R. L. Stevenson a half century before, commented on the filth and poisonous atmosphere of the trains they were on. The Union Pacific cars, said R. L. S., had begun to stink abominably after the ninety-hour journey from Omaha to Ogden, Utah: "Our nostrils were assailed by rancid air...a whiff of pure menagerie, only a little sourer, as from men instead of monkeys."[18]

The Chinese, who were in separate cars on Stevenson's train, smelled far better than the Europeans and Americans who never washed on the train. In spite of great difficulties, the Orientals kept themselves clean. As for the Canadian harvest trains, while most excursionists did not complain of dirt or bad air in the cars, Frank Parker Day referred to it. Peter M. Campbell of Red Islands boarded a harvest train in the province of Quebec. He was soon disgusted by the dirt and slovenly behaviour of the passengers. Angus Beaton of Mabou never had a bath from the time he left Nova Scotia until he returned. In Day's car, by the way, only the Cape Breton miners were careful about keeping themselves clean. As for the farms on which harvesters eventually found themselves, bathing facilities were nearly non-existent, or at least not available to the workers unless they could find a suitable slough.

In the interviews for this book, harvesters rarely mentioned dirt and bad air. Yet many of those men must have felt a bit "antsy" on arriving in Winnipeg after days of confinement on the trains.

And hardly ever, except for a few sensational incidents, was their any chance to relieve sexual urges en route. Indeed many felt an irresistible desire to interrupt their journey when they stretched their muscles on the station platform in Winnipeg. And the fleshpots were close at hand. Bars and brothels a-plenty dotted Main Street north and south of the CPR station. On the westward journey, of course, many of them, short of cash, had to sublimate their urges by wrestling sheaves of grain. On the way home with their summer's earnings, however, they were beset by "an awesome assortment of con men, sneak thieves, pickpockets and pimps" waiting to separate the travellers from their cash.[19]

CHAPTER 4

Outward Bound
Voices from
the Harvest Excursions

"**I** WENT ON FOUR HARVEST EXCURSIONS from Sydney, beginning in 1922 when I was seventeen. The first year the train was orderly. In 1923 Cape Bretoners that were hitting the bottle got off at Antigonish and started kissing women on the platform. They kissed a couple of girls that were saying goodbye to boys going on the excursion. A brawl broke out, but sober Cape Bretoners broke it up. I learned on this trip that the Cape Bretoners had been branded as wild men, savages, roughnecks, since Year One. Now the rest of the trip was quiet. A lot of poker was played and a couple of card sharks thrown out, but no harm done.

In August 1924 I went out again. There were a good many fights among Cape Bretoners from different towns until we hooked on to the harvest train at Saint John. After that we stuck together like glue. We had lots of Demarara rum.

Somewhere in Ontario, at a water stop, the boys threw stones at a house that looked empty. A man came out with a pistol and fired at us. There was a mad scramble for cover. The Mounties went over to the house, stayed a while, then came back and laid down the law to the harvesters. In North Bay the train stopped for two hours or so, with a hotbox. The Cape Bretoners ran wild. They wrecked a pool parlour, one fellow smashed a big wall clock with a pool ball. I was playing traffic cop on the street. By the time the Mounties and local cops came we were all in the train and pulling out."

"**I LEFT SYDNEY MINES** in 1927 with two buddies. I was twenty years old. Some men had no tickets—they hid under seats or behind luggage when conductors came through. We had to watch our luggage in the luggage rack or it would be stolen. When the train got to Truro there was a big fight on the platform. I sat on top of the train to watch it.

Before reaching Montreal the boys stole all the goods the newsboy had for sale—two thousand dollars' worth, somebody said—and sold it themselves. RCMP got on the train every now and then, looking for thieves. They never caught anyone.

Before we reached Winnipeg most of the seats were thrown out.

Somebody pulled a gun and shot a horse at one stop. Another place they drained a lot of cider barrels."

"**IN 1912 WE HAD TO STAY** on the train in Quebec. The harvesters on a train ahead had looted, raped and raised hell. Sheriff and armed police kept us on the train."

"**I WENT ALONE IN 1920**, twenty-seven years old. I had to borrow the fare from an old bachelor neighbour. He was reluctant to give it to me—thought I'd got my girl in trouble and was shipping out. I convinced him otherwise, he gave me the fare—twenty-four dollars and six dollars extra. My parents were against me going, and they had no money anyway. I caught the excursion train at Oxford Junction. We had to change cars in Montreal—our car had something go wrong with it. Two years later my girl—then my wife—had our honeymoon trip on the harvest excursion train!"

"**I** WENT OUT IN 1912, after teaching school for several years. I knew I would get four times as much salary in the West. Some other women were on the train, quite a few, in fact. The CPR put a nice car with cushioned seats on the tail end of the train for the women. It was nice. But the men were uncivilized in the other cars. They smashed windows out of the train and caused a commotion every time we stopped."

"**T**HREE OF US TOOK THE CPR excursion train out of Saint John in 1925. It was a very quiet trip. There were no Mounties or other police on the train, and no women."

"**A** YOUNG MAN from Pictou County, Nova Scotia, obtained his harvest excursion fare in a somewhat devious fashion. We'll call him Will Ross though it was not exactly his name. Will, at eighteen years of age, wanted money. His skinflint father, Ebenezeer, refused to pay him for his labours, thinking it enough to provide him with his bed and board. 'All Right!' Will announced, 'I'm hitting the harvest excursion!'

'Ah, Will, Will,' Eb moaned (lying through his teeth was Eb), 'but if you'll stay home and help us get the crop and the firewood in I'll see that you're well rewarded. I had the grey mare bred; there'll be a colt in the spring. If you stay home this year you can have that colt next year and do whatever you want with it.'

Somewhat satisfied, Will stayed home, worked like a dog at the hay, the grain, the turnips and the wood, then left to work in the foundry in New Glasgow for the winter. In July he came home and inquired about the colt. 'Ah yes,' said Eb, rolling his eyes, 'the colt! Well, you see, it was a splendid colt and Rory McMaster offered me a big price for it, so I sold it.' No word of money for the son.

Will was not pleased. He had saved some of his meagre earnings but needed more money to get a proper outfit for the trip west. And he had inherited some of old Eb's devious ways. He went to New Glasgow with the mail driver and bought, among other things, a high quality woolen overcoat at Spiro's clothing store. His father admired the coat when Will arrived home from shopping. 'My, my, Will! That's a grand coat! It would keep me nice and warm when I'm taking long trips with the pung sleigh in the winter. Could I try it on?'

Now Will and his father were both stocky, broadchested, big-shouldered gorillas. Eb found the coat a. perfect fit. 'Well now, boy, will you sell me that coat?' 'Well, okay, I guess so. But it cost me seventy-five dollars.' After some grumbling Eb came across with the cash. Will set off on the harvest train three days later.

At the end of the month Eb got a bill for seventy-five dollars from the clothing store. Will had charged the coat to his father's account.**"**

"I WENT OUT IN 1903 with my brother. Some men off the train wrecked a picnic stand when we stopped one place. Another place they stole cheese from a workman's shanty and we helped eat it. There were some women on the train, going to teach school in the West. **"**

"I WENT WEST when the war started—1914—and the next year too. Jobs were scarce here, and everybody was either joining up or going west. I was too young for the army, didn't want to be completely left out of things, so I went west. In 1914 when we got on the train at Fredericton Junction we saw one car loaded with Nova Scotians, all locked up, on the tail end of the train. They were all drunk, were never allowed in our car.

We had a twenty-minute stop every hundred miles or so to change engines. People at the stops had refreshment booths set up, were ringing bells to encourage us to come and buy. At White River the boys set out to raid a liquor store. Two men with revolvers put them out. But they smashed the store windows with rocks. Tied a pung sled to the train too. **"**

"WE GOT ON THE REGULAR TRAIN at Alba, paid full fare to Moncton. Had to stay in Moncton overnight in a hotel crawling with bedbugs. It was 1917—I had just turned seventeen.

There were at least seven hundred people on board the excursion train; we needed a pusher engine for the hills, and often we had to wait a long time for the pusher.

There were fights, some of them real bad, after the gang raided liquor stores in Quebec. They stole metal tubs and buckets from other stores and beat on them like drums. Somebody stole a bunch of hens from a chicken farm and let them go loose in the train. The women screamed at that more than at the fights. Some men from the mining towns carried revolvers, I remember. They took a cow from a poor French woman and tried to put it on the train. Police and priests tried to reason with them at some stops but the harvesters only laughed at them. There were no police on the train. I remember seeing a woman at one stop sitting by her house with a rifle across her knees. Nobody bothered her."

"**FIVE TRIPS I MADE** to the harvest fields between '21 and '26. Went for adventure the first year, then for the money.

Twenty-five of us went from McGivney Junction in 1921. There were enough married couples to have a separate 'married car' at Fredericton Junction. Twenty dollars and a half was the fare to Winnipeg, twenty-five dollars return if you'd work a month at harvesting. Tickets were transferable between CN and CP.

Trouble on the train? No, not a bit! We had lots of music—fiddler and harmonica players. Our train stopped at Cochrane on Sunday and all hands went to church. We had to wait in Cochrane—Winnipeg was full of harvesters and our train was held in Cochrane. At the station we had a twelve-piece orchestra going and some great stepdancing.

Plenty of poker games on the train, sometimes eight hundred dollars on the table. There were CN cops and Mounties on the train.

Well, there was a little trouble one place in Ontario. A Chinaman was operating a store and lunch counter. A harvester didn't like a custard pie that he had bought—he threw it at the Chinaman after a little argument. The Chinaman threw a pie back, the harvester ducked, and the pie landed slap in the face of a Mountie coming in the door. To avenge the honour of the Mounted Police the harvesters wrecked the place and ran the poor Chinaman off into the woods."

"IN 1928, THE LAST OF ALL EXCURSIONS, I was on. Two fellows with me. We caught the train in Moncton; it was already loaded with New Brunswick and Prince Edward Island people. The Nova Scotians were on another train. There would have been hell to pay if they had all been on the same train. A bunch of women going out to teach school were in a car of their own, guarded by police at night. There was one honeymoon couple on the train. No rough stuff on the train. A few stores were raided in Ontario, but most were boarded up."

"MY BROTHER AND I WENT WEST on the CPR out of Fredericton in 1915. I was twenty years old. Twelve dollars to Winnipeg, one half a cent a mile from there out. There were Cape Bretoners on the train, they caused some trouble. Stole bananas from a store, kicked a gum dispenser off a wall. There were no police on the train, and the railway police at stations seemed frightened. In one place where we stopped for water in Ontario, some Cape Bretoners went up to an Indian hut, said something to an Indian woman there. An Indian man came out of the hut with a rifle and fired over their heads. They left in a rush. But on the New Brunswick car we were civilized."

"I WAS SEVENTEEN YEARS OLD, had my Grade Ten Certificate and a license to teach. I had taught in Fairmont for ninety dollars a year, had to fight to get it. In the West I was offered ninety dollars a month! A number of other girls went out with me from Antigonish in 1917. Very quiet on the train; no police that I saw, no need of them. But oh my! There was trouble when the train stopped at a place in Northern Ontario! Some of the boys started to get off; big whiskery men came out of buildings near the station and started shooting. Somebody shouted: 'Look out, it's the Doukhobors!' One young man who got off the train first was shot and killed. The others carried him back on, with bullets flying around them. We could hear bullets striking the train. We left there in a hurry— the conductor must have signalled the engineer.

The poor fellow who was killed was only a boy. We took up a collection on the train to ship his body back home."

"**WHY DID I GO OUT** on the harvest? Well now, I would say it was to make some money and to see the country. It only cost about twelve dollars to Winnipeg in 1909, and a little more to come back if you worked at the grain long enough.

We took supplies—canned goods, chicken hard-cooked, cookies and crackers—on board—we knew there'd be no grub on the train. We took blankets too, as it could get chilly at night. Very quiet trip from Fredericton Junction, no rough stuff at all. But we heard a train of harvesters had raised hell the year before both on the train and at every stop."

"**I HAD BEEN WORKING** in a hotel in Saint John in 1911 when I decided to go west with a neighbour from Gagetown, a man named Dunn. The train was so crowded we had to sleep in the smoker. We couldn't get any hot food, as the old-timers kept us away from the stove. Very quiet trip. I remember, though, the train crew coming through at night to check tickets. I complained at being awakened and one told me: 'Shut up, young fella, or I'll beat yer God-damned head off!' ''

"**T**HERE WAS NO SEPARATE CAR for women on the train I rode to Winnipeg in 1920. I was with some other girls from Rexton going out to teach school. There was no noise or rough stuff on our train. The train ahead of us, though, had raided and ransacked along the line in Quebec, and we were not allowed off the train there."

"**O**NE DOLLAR A DAY working in the New Brunswick woods, four to seven dollars a day on the harvest! That's why I went out west in '20, '21 and '22. I went always CP one way, CN on return, to see more of Canada. My three trips were quiet and peaceable. No women, no police either. Mind you, the crew might wake you up anytime to check your ticket. And the harvesters would all get off to eat at station restaurants, then rush out without paying."

"**F**IVE OF US TOOK THE TRAIN at Iona, Cape Breton, in July 1928. Just about my first train trip. Those colonist cars were crowded! Generally it was a quiet trip, though some Glace Bay boys were fond of scrapping. I saw no women on the train. By the way, you didn't visit other cars—it might be dangerous."

"**I** TELL YOU, SIR, the excursion train was the longest passenger train I ever did see—twenty-three coaches out of Fredericton Junction. One car at the rear was full of women. We never saw them except through the windows. What year? 1923 it was; I was eighteen, and my father was with me. No fightin' or rumpus or anything on our train, I guess. There were four black men that played a lot of poker, made a good pile of money, I expect. Well now! At Allanwater we stopped quite a while. There was an Indian encampment in sight, and some of the men got off the train to have a squint at it. All the Indians able to run made for the woods. Nobody was left but some old women, all holding axes or knives."

"**I WENT OUT IN '26.** Liked it so well I went back in '27, stayed out and homesteaded. Both train trips were very quiet.

Well, there was a store looted in Ontario and ten men were arrested for that by the Mounted Police in Winnipeg. But there was never any fighting.

I think the stories of wild Cape Breton men are exaggerated. But they are clannish—they hid some of their Cape Breton crowd, who had no tickets, when the train crew came through. One peg-legged man from Cape Breton got right to Winnipeg with no ticket."

"**T**IMES WERE SLACK in Trenton in 1925—the steelworks were only working three or four days a week. The boss said our jobs were guaranteed on return if we went on the harvest. About thirty of us from around Trenton went that year. I had a suitcase full of grub—cooked chicken and that sort of thing. There were a lot of women aboard, mostly schoolteachers, some cooks. No rough stuff, except that one man threw a whiskey bottle through a window after he had emptied it."

"**I** STARTED OUT IN 1924, but we were turned back at New Glasgow station: there wasn't enough grain in the West and no more harvesters were needed. I went the next year. Quiet enough, though a local drunk tried to raise a stink. He had a pistol, kept hitting people with it. We knew he had no bullets, so we took it from him, tossed it out the window. Sure calmed him down.

I went out again in '26. Not much rough stuff on the train.

Ach, there were some women got off the train at Winnipeg station who were nearly trampled by wild men from Cape Breton and P. E. Island. I helped protect them until the police came."

"**A** BUDDY AND I WENT OUT in '27 and again in '28. Good chance to get extra money and see the country. A few women teachers were aboard, going out to take over schools in the West. Big train—seventeen cars out of Truro. We had a cook car—you could get a lunch on the train. No fighting or anything, though some men got off one morning and kicked a lot of garbage cans around. Yes, we had Cape Bretoners aboard, but they were quite peaceable. In '27 Mounties got on the train at Quebec—there was no raiding after that!"

"**F**IVE OF US YOUNG FELLOWS went from Antigonish in '26 and '27.

In Nova Scotia we were getting twenty-five cents an hour for a nine-hour day working on the road. We finished making hay in Lakevale, then took the early excursion train in July. I heard a trainman say there were over twelve hundred passengers aboard. There was one carload of schoolteachers—women—and another of people suffering from asthma who hoped for relief in the West.

Some of the Glace Bay and Sydney fellows did a bit of smashing on the train. Nobody got aboard after

New Glasgow, by the way. Five railroad cops were aboard, doing nothing that I could see. A lot of harvesters raided stores in Ontario."

"**I** GOT ON THE TRAIN at Point Tupper with four others. Had to stand up as far as New Glasgow, where another car was attached. There was a bad bunch aboard—there were three or four fights every day. No policemen on until redcoated Mounties got on at Winnipeg. 1928 it was. There were 934 passengers—I asked the conductor in Winnipeg. And that did not take in the bums with no tickets that hid when the crew came around.

Past the Lakehead a man came with a covered wagon to sell ice cream and stuff. The bunch off the train unhitched the horse, threw the man and cart over a pile of poles! One man had his head split open by a thrown bottle. But I don't recall many broken windows."

"**T**HERE WERE A FEW WOMEN on the train that three other fellows and I took out of Pictou in 1920. Yes, there was some fighting and raiding. Railway police did nothing. I had the promise of a job in the West before leaving home, through a man who had been out in '19 but couldn't go in '20.

We went again in '22. Very quiet trip. There were two Mounted Policemen—twin brothers—on our train. Two Frenchmen, a big one from Quebec and a small one from New Brunswick, got to fighting in our car. The big guy pulled a revolver. A Mountie did a handspring over a seat and knocked the gun up so the bullet went through the roof. At the next stop he took the two Frenchmen off and had them fight it out in a ring formed around them by other harvesters. The little Maritimer beat the shit out of the big Quebecer and everybody cheered."

"**My FIRST EXCURSION IN 1919**, well, it was a real donnybrook. Cape Bretoners smashed the windows out, they raided a barbershop in Ontario, taking scissors, razors, smocks on the train. Mounties were aboard the train the other years, and things were quiet."

"**Twenty-FIVE AND '26 WERE THE YEARS** that I went. Twenty dollars and twenty cents, Fredericton Junction to Winnipeg. A car from the East was hooked onto our car. One of our New Brunswick boys got some liquor in him, wanted to fight somebody. None of us felt like scrapping. He went back to this other car, came crawling back with his face smashed in—'My God!' he said, 'those are wild men from Cape Breton back there!'

There were Mounties on the train, watching the women's car. They kept a fellow from taking a stolen cow onto the train. In '25 there was an old fellow waiting with a bakery wagon at one stop. The harvesters pushed him aside, unharnessed the horse and took all his goods. He and the horse just stood back and let them be—didn't squawk or anything. So they took up a collection and paid him well."

"**In 1925 THERE WAS A CARLOAD** of schoolteachers on the train and two CNR policemen. We got on in Boisdale, Cape Breton. At one stop the boys caught a bull and chained him to the rear of the train. His horns pulled off when the train started. At another place they tied a mowing machine on. It blew up when she started off—may have been the first steel on the moon! Stole blueberries and cream from a farmer in Quebec too. It wasn't safe to go to sleep on the train—you'd be 'decorated' or half-murdered."

"**I** WENT BY MYSELF, in 1928—I was twenty years old. I expected to earn good money—four dollars a day, with a dollar bonus for good work. The crowd was mostly Cape Bretoners. No fights or rough stuff at all, plenty music and song. There were some women in the car I was in, one of them an old woman who had her three grandchildren with her. In one town where we stopped in Ontario all the stores were closed and boarded up—the train ahead of us had raised hell. The grandmother was out of grub for her kids. I talked to a man on a side street. He took me to a merchant who opened the back door of his shop, sold me bread and milk and butter and gave me a bottle of jam for the children.

In another town a young policeman stood up where all could see him and asked the harvesters to spare the town. 'I'm only one', says he, 'and there's a whole crowd of you. I might shoot one or two, but the rest would get me. Now these are fine people here, working people, and I'm asking you not to hurt my town. People have been good to me here.' The Cape Bretoners took him up on their shoulders and carried him around the street then. They would have killed anyone who did any damage there."

"**W**E WENT OUT the northern route, on the CNR. There were two brothers aboard, who got on in Antigonish. Real hard-case characters. When we got to Quebec, they'd get out long black cloaks, broad floppy hats and Roman collars they likely stole somewhere. Up and down the 'priests' paraded on the station platform, begging money from Quebec people 'for the missions.' Then they spent the money on beer. That was right after the war. Dunno their names—the others called them 'The Cobalts.'

One time our train stopped out in the country in Quebec—we could see a peg-leg man and a little boy working around a woodpile. A mob of harvesters jumped the train and headed for them. The poor Frenchman made for the house, likely praying. But the harvesters didn't bother him—they grabbed axes and saws and lit into the woodpile, sawing and splitting. The poor cripple was out trying to thank them— they had a whole lot of wood cut—when the train whistle blew. Most of the crowd ran for the train, but three of them damned Cape Bretoners grabbed the poor old fellow, stretched him out on the sawhorse, and sawed off his wooden leg.**"**

"I WAS WORKING on a cruising party with International Paper in Gaspé and New Brunswick in the summer of 1927. I didn't want to go to Newfoundland when the job finished—I was going back to college soon—so I was fired. I joined the harvest excursion in Halifax the middle of August. Fare was thirty dollars to Winnipeg. Eight hundred men and two women were on the train. Soon after we pulled out some young devils threw the stove lids out the windows. We stopped in Truro. Some men went hunting for a bootlegger, and by the way they acted later they must have found one. In Quebec a crew went to another bootlegger. Foolishly he took them to the shack where he kept his rum. They bought a bottle or two, then smashed in the door and took all the rest.

In North Bay there were men waiting on the platform with cases of prohibition beer—4.4%. They broke into the cases with axes and sold it to harvesters. On the train, after drinking a few bottles they found they weren't getting drunk—the stuff was weak. So they threw bottles out the windows. Later we slowed down at a siding where a gang of section men were standing, hands behind their backs. One of our crowd threw a bottle at them. But the section men had both hands full of rocks, and it wasn't long before our windows came crashing in. At another stop the harvesters saw six pigs coming down the road—pigs of about seventy-five pounds. Seven hundred men started chasing the pigs, often getting upset when a pig ran between their feet. Eventually they took one on the train, but I don't know what happened to it.

The Cape Breton train was running ahead of ours. We usually had two or three Cape Bretoners on our train. They would fall off or get left behind. Then they'd come in with us until we reached a place where they could get back where they belonged. We pulled into Winnipeg alongside the Cape Breton train—I don't think there was a window left in it."

"**A**BOUT A MONTH OR SO BEFORE each excursion they put up posters advertising it in church halls and livery stables and on telephone poles. We were supposed to get a cheap trip to Winnipeg and see the country. Most of us had never been past Antigonish in the east and New Glasgow in the west—not me, anyways. Offered high wages too—four dollars a day for stooking—that's piling them bouquets on end—and five for threshing. Times were hard in Nova Scotia—well, we didn't suffer much want, but we didn't have much riches. But when we went west, it was a different story—they had prosperity!

I left school when I shouldn't have—took off my

schoolbag and hung it on a post. And went to work rolling logs off the brow at Fulton's Mill. I wasn't too welcome when I got home that night! I got three dollars a day at Fulton's Mill and boarded at home— pretty good money here in the early '20s."

"**A** COUSIN AND I BOARDED the excursion train in Amherst in 1925. Crowded train. Twenty dollars to Winnipeg. One Cape Breton car, one ladies' car. Rip-roaring good time—music and song. Fights? Lord, no! We travelled from one end of the train to the other, met lots of nice people. There were railroad cops on, they had no work to do."

"**P**EOPLE BOARDED THE TRAIN right to Rivière-du-Loup. We crossed the Quebec bridge. Only one incident I remember on the train. A sixteen-year-old boy from Westchester was trying to get to Winnipeg with no ticket—his friends hid him under seats and that sort of thing. A conductor finally found him, said he would put him off at the next stop. The boy's friends cornered Mr. Conductor, said if he put the kid off, they'd throw him off the train when it was moving. The boy got to Winnipeg.

When we got to Cochrane, Ontario, we found the stores all closed. We were getting pretty hungry. There was a beer parlour open, though—a bunch of us went in and filled up on 4.4% beer.

Finally the RCMP got a merchant to open the door of his store. He put a desk across the door, sold us grub across the desk, wouldn't let us in the store. Well, we had a piper from Cape Breton on the train, a great fellow. He piped us through the streets and we spread piles of pulp wood all over the streets. Good enough for a town where people were so unfriendly!

Railroad cars that brought the harvest excursionists to the West. Top: The Colonist car of the Canadian National Railway *(Courtesy National Archives of Canada)* and, below that, the Emigrant Sleeper car of the Intercolonial Railway *(Courtesy Provincial Archives of New Brunswick)*. Below: Inside one of the first CPR colonist-class cars *(Courtesy Canadian Pacific Railway Archives)*.

The arrival of harvest excursionists at the Winnipeg railway station, Canadian Pacific Railway, in 1897. *(Courtesy Provincial Archives of Manitoba)*. Below: Interior of Emigrant car *(Courtesy Provincial Archives of New Brunswick)*.

The next time we went, we went CPR. We were held up for a while—somebody on an excursion train ahead of us had heaved a bottle through a window and killed a girl on the regular passenger train. He was never found, of course—nobody dared squeal if they knew."

"**I WAS ONE OF A CROWD OF GIRLS** that took the train at Scotsburn in August 1910. A big crowd to see us off. We were going out to teach—everybody wanted to go west.

I had a big new trunk and lots of dresses. I'd been teaching four years and had money in the bank. You could buy a skirt at Baillie's in Pictou for seventy-five cents, and a big hat for a dollar fifty. No slacks or short skirts. We were well covered—black stockings and all. We took blankets, pillows, and a supply of food. We had mouth organ players and one harvester with a violin—there was plenty of music. At one stop in Ontario, though, where a store had been looted by harvesters before, someone knocked on our windows and warned us about the angry townspeople. 'Don't get out! They've got guns and are ready to shoot!' So we stayed on the train."

"**ME, I WAS WORKING** at the coal face when I was only sixteen. I went west in '26—I was nineteen years old, wanted to see the West after hearing so much from fellows who had been out. We left from Sydney. The windows were all out of the coaches when we got to Truro. There were rum sellers at every station, booze flowing everywhere. When we got into Quebec the train began by stopping at stations. We'd get off and beat up all the Frenchmen we could find. The bastards had hid in the woods while our boys

were slaughtered in France, after all. After we'd clob-
bered all we could find the cops would put us back on
the train. After a while, until we got to Winnipeg, we
only stopped to change engines."

"**W**E BEGAN THE 1924 TREK in Sydney, hooked
on to the CPR harvest train in Saint John. Things
were quiet enough on the train except that three men
who were playing cards in the other end of the car got
in a hook with a young fellow—a neighbour of mine
from Caledonia—I think he caught 'em cheating. They
were rough characters from the Northside. The boy
came and hid behind me. One big fellow who was
chasing him took a swing at me. I ducked under his
roundhouse right, beat him the length of the car, and
knocked him out through the door at the end of the
car. They didn't bother us any more. At North Bay
some harvesters went in a bar and wrecked a nice
grandfather clock there. The other people on the train
did not like that.

There were plenty of young fellows from Glace
Bay and other mining districts on the train. They
didn't go west because they had no jobs, they believed
it was in their own interest to help harvest the grain
crop. We had several young men from the British-
Canadian Cooperative stores who had got leave of ab-
sence to work on the harvest. We had a young person-
able Mountie on the train out. His name was Verge.
One reason there was no trouble on the train was that
guy, he got along fine with everybody."

"**N**OVA SCOTIA and Prince Edward Island men
were a wild bunch. On the three trips I made west in
the late '20s they always caused trouble. One trip the
train stopped near Edmundston and a bunch went to

a place they could buy liquor. Police seized a lot of their booze as they boarded the train. When the train was pulling out a regular barrage of empty bottles sailed through the windows at seven cops on the platform. Most of them missed, but the harvesters meant well. They stuffed toilet paper down toilet bowls until the stuff was all under and over the cars. One place where we stopped in Ontario a man was digging a basement. The harvesters pushed a wagon load of rocks into the basement. He let loose a Husky dog that bit some of them. Another place they tried to pull an Indian dog apart. An Indian woman—likely it was her dog—let loose at them with a shotgun. Some of them were a bit heavier when they reached the train with lead in their asses."

Leaving Antigonish station on the harvest train excursion. Left to right, sitting: Dan Beaton, Dan "Decket" MacGillivray. Front row: Dan J. Grant, Morristown; Peter Smith, Arisaig; Dan C. MacNeil, Lakevale; Vincent J. MacDonald and Alex MacNaughton, Antigonish; Louis Meehan, Fairmont; Anthony Murphy, New Glasgow.

CHAPTER 5

Finding Work
Teachers and Farmhands

FRANK PARKER DAY had no intention of working at the harvest in 1920. He wanted the experience of riding the excursion train and the chance to travel west at a low price. He visited his sister in Winnipeg and probably viewed grain fields only at a distance. A young man from Bear River who sat with him had just completed high school. He intended to study at Normal School in Alberta and teach in the West. Several women on the train, respectable and well-dressed, were obviously schoolteachers. Some other women, hungry and ill-clothed, Day called "bedraggled creatures" going west with no preparation and no clear objectives. Wilfred Creighton saw women of the same type on his train in the '20s. Women had worked in the fields during World War I when labour was desperately short, but the experiment was not repeated.

Most women passengers on the excursion were going out to teach in prairie schools. Mrs. Elliott of Barker's Point, New Brunswick, made the trip in 1920 with three other girls from Rexton. A quiet trip; men and women were not segregated as in some trains. Mrs. Elliott's aunt in Regina had found a position for her in a one-room school where all the fifty students were German or Scandinavian. "Such strange names!"

she recalled. But they were a congenial lot—she stayed there four years. Aside from weekends the only holiday was Christmas Day. Her predecessor in that school—an Ontario girl "from the city"—had become so lonely she had to leave the job.

Elizabeth Creighton Shaw from West River, Pictou County, went to Alberta in 1918 to see her two sisters who had gone west on the harvest train the previous year. After nursing victims of the flu epidemic, she went teaching in Edmonton. There she earned sixty dollars a month. In Lime Rock, Nova Scotia, she had been paid 115 dollars a year plus a small government grant.

Mrs. Elliott received a thousand dollars a year in Saskatchewan; in New Brunswick she had to make do with 337 dollars. Selina MacGillivray of Antigonish enjoyed an even larger inflation of her salary from one hundred dollars a year in Fairmont—which she had to fight to get—to ninety dollars a *month* in Saskatchewan. Selina had no trouble getting her pay in the West, but Elizabeth Shaw had to sue the trustees to get hers in the Peace River country.

A. H. MacKay, Nova Scotia's Superintendent of Education, deplored the low salaries paid in the East compared to the Prairies. In 1904 male teachers in the Maritimes were averaging 240 dollars a year while females took home 195 dollars. Their counterparts on the Prairies received 420 dollars and 432 dollars.[1] In the Maritime Provinces public schools were run and financed by municipal or local governments with some aid from the provinces—provinces whose public income was sadly diminished by their entering Confederation. In the West, public schools were financed by the sale of land, and a very large fund was built up for school costs as settlement increased.[2]

So the rapid expansion of prairie settlement created new employment opportunities every year for teachers, opportunities further improved by the "mortality rate" or marriage rate, which was extremely high on the bachelor-infested plains. Single men, starved for feminine company, besieged the teacherage or boarding house. Eight or ten hopeful swains would "drop in" every Sunday afternoon. Barry Broadfoot was told, "We never had a teacher last more than a year" before succumbing to matrimony. One only lasted three months. An eighteen-year-old woman from Nova Scotia did not even have to leave the school to get her man. A sixteen-year-old male pupil stayed after hours to clean the school. Extracurricular activity resulted in pregnancy; the two were married, had five more children in a few years.[3]

Whether by law, convention or custom, married women could not teach school on the Prairies, at least in Saskatchewan. But no such restriction was placed on males: H. M. MacDonald, Antigonish, and Ed Campbell, East Lake Ainslie, continued in the classroom after succumbing to matrimony. As with the homesteading law, this was another example of discrimination.

Mention of discrimination brings up another reason many young teachers had to leave the Maritimes. In the industrial areas, an old labour man declared, miners' children or labourers' children could not get positions: trustees, councillors, merchants, and mine officials used their influence to secure the job for their own children or those of relatives. Even if a miner's daughter had done well in Normal School, she had to go west for the two years of experience required to get a position.[4]

Many teachers had secured teaching positions before leaving home. Jane MacKay believed she had a school when she took the train out to Winnipeg in 1910, having reached there on the harvest train with ten other teachers. But the Teachers' Agency in Regina mistakenly sent a girl from Regina to take the same one-room school. The school trustee who met the train had to make a fast decision when two teachers for the one-room school at Badger Hill faced him on the station platform. The other girl told him she was from Regina. Jane said, "I'm from Pictou County, Nova Scotia!" The trustee pointed his cigar at the girl from away Down East: "You've come furthest," he announced, "I'll take you!"[5]

SOME OF THE "FARMING" HARVESTERS already had employment when arriving in Winnipeg. Others took a chance on going where they heard crops were good. There they went to grain elevators, asked local businessmen or policemen where workers were wanted, or—very rarely—used employment agents. Steve MacNeil from Big Pond was footsore by the time he found an employer:

"Three excursion trains hit Winnipeg at the same time. Terrible crowded! Two MacIsaacs and I went to Regina. The harvest wasn't ready; the town was full of men looking for work. A man came up to us: 'You fellows new here?' We said, 'Yes.' The MacIsaacs were hired first; the Newfies and I stayed in one room at a Chinaman's hotel. Ran out of money—we slept under the station platform next night. We walked for miles looking for work. I got on with a farmer—E. S. Dennis—married to a teacher from Truro. Great place!"

In 1911, Abner Belyea and a friend from Gagetown, New Brunswick, paid one dollar each to an employment agent in Winnipeg who promised a job. The

New Brunswick men didn't like the farmer's looks. Abner lit a paper, stopped a northbound train, and went to Solsgirth. There he got a job with an English farmer who had come up from the States—"Too damn many Germans there."

Stan Mason, broke in Winnipeg, used his last thirty-five cents for a bag of candy to ward off starvation. Some of his buddies pooled the little money they had, went to Maryfield, Saskatchewan, slept in the station all night. They got a job with a Scotch farmer, who pronounced the two Nova Scotians "the best men he ever had." Arthur Rae from Dumfries, New Brunswick, went on to Vanguard in 1923, was hired by a farmer at the railway station.

In 1919, W. F. MacInnis of Lyons Brook went to Unity, Saskatchewan, and encountered a farmer at the station looking for men. A. D. Grant and three other Pictou men had their jobs guaranteed before leaving home through one of their number who was a veteran harvester. In 1914, Henry R. Thompson found work through an employment agent in Regina. Bill Campbell, in 1925, was hired by a man coming through the branch-line train calling for workers. Archie MacIvor from Baddeck found a German farmer who looked like Kaiser Bill—this was in 1917—at Moose Jaw. The German hired Archie and four other men for his farm near Drinkwater.

Archie and his chums tried to sleep on a scaffold in the barn where they rolled around on sheaves of grain all night in spite of heavy horse blankets weighting them down. Another Baddeck man—Joe MacDonald—slept in a bunkhouse. Dan Hugh MacInnis from Antigonish was in clover, sleeping in the farmhouse on a feather bed. A. B. MacIsaac had a good bunk while working for Irish farmers at Cars-land, Alberta. But at another place the bunks were crawling with lice. Dan Allan Gillis left a farm because of lice, found good accommodations with another farmer. Ernie Gourley slept on an iron bed in the granary. Lee Goodwin of Kingsport recalled sleeping in a rough bunkhouse in 1920; later that year he was in a box stall in the barn.

More fortunate was Jim Murray from Black Point: Belgian farmers had him sleep in their house, treated him very well, cried when he left to go home. Dr. Walter Chestnutt, when a harvester, slept in a big tent during the 1917 harvest, "arising at 5:30 A.M. to the sound of coyotes."[6]

Travelling between farms, John Annesley spent a poor night in a leaky roadside shack, another night in a motorcar. On another occasion John and a buddy came by chance on a loft above an empty stable. There were some blankets there, which should have made them suspicious. At two in the morning they were evicted by two teamsters returning from a long haul with some stock. They spent the rest of the night in less comfort in the stable.[7]

In *Many Trails*, a splendid account of life in Western Canada, R. D. Symons recalls:

"Bed meant unrolling your blankets wherever you could be snug. Haylofts, empty granaries (hard floors there!), feed alleys in barns, the lee of a straw stack burrowed in—all these and various other places I have slept in. One's fatigue soon overcame the discomfort of the couch...."[8]

R. D. SYMONS' LITTLE BOOK contains a very good description of harvest operations; a whole chapter is devoted to the subject. But in the account Mr. Symons—himself a Westerner, by adoption at least—

neglects to mention one item that brought pain, suffering, and embarrassment to thousands of tenderfeet from the East. Even after a half century many old harvesters could not speak of the prairie water—drinking water—without lapsing into a spate of sulphurous invective. "Like Epsom salts mixed with soap," Louis Hall recalled, "that's what the damn stuff tasted like. And it reamed you out like liquid dynamite!"

Alfred MacKay from Big Harbour, Cape Breton, gave the stuff full credit for curing his appendicitis attacks. "Nothing, *nothing* could lodge in any gut following one draught of alkali water in Saskatchewan. It sure kept the decks cleared for the next meal!"[9]

D. N. Brodie found the water "fairly clear" but it "smelled like an old wash tub and tasted of soap."[10] John Neil Campbell compared the smell to that of boiling pit socks. "Terrible drinking water!" Lorne Robson recalled. "It was poison to most of the Easterners. It was like drinking a glass of Epsom salts. The drugstores did a landslide business selling extract of wild strawberry."[11]

Besides the strawberry extract, lime juice or cream of tartar could be added to water to neutralize the alkali. But some Easterners—unable to stand the violent purging—had to go home. Indeed some tenderfeet died from the vicious combination of heat and dysentery, the latter brought on by alkali water.[12] Harvesters were sometimes disgusted at finding maggots or tadpoles in the water. D. J. Campbell of New Glasgow condemned the water in Manitoba as:

"Wretched...the workmen could not be induced to drink it, even in the fields, where they were toiling and perspiring under the rays of a sun, hot for a time as in the tropics. Stagnant water, which is at the same time brackish, is no allurement, even to the thirsty."[13]

Maritimers were used to a plentiful supply of good water, still relatively pure and unpolluted. Prairie farmers paid out large sums of money to have deep wells drilled, and were pardonably proud of the product, having built up an immunity. But for the boys from the East—well, James Minifie expressed profound sympathy with them: "enduring diarrhea in a region bereft of toilet facilities, squatting at night in a field of stubble qualifies for Dante's *Purgatorio*."[14]

APART FROM THE WATER and terrific heat, there were few insuperable difficulties for Easterners as far as the work was concerned. If properly garbed, with hat, leather gloves, overalls or coveralls, and boots, any healthy harvester used to manual labour could stand the gaff. Miners, woodsmen, fishermen, and farm workers adapted to the working conditions quickly.

Sedentary workers had a worse time, especially if not used to horses. Even those accustomed to working with quiet old Dobbin at home could have trouble with half-broken prairie nags. And there were unexpected problems: a few harvesters working for German farmers found it impossible to make the beasts understand them: they had not discovered the beauty of bilingualism and obeyed only German commands. Occasionally a man with no horse experience would lie about it in order to get hired. One such was found trying to get a horse to walk forward into the collar like an ox walking into a yoke. This almost makes credible Gus MacNeil's story of the English greenhorn swearing in the stable: "I can't get this thing over the beast's 'ead, is bally eahs ahh frozen!" He was trying to put a bridle on a cow.

Stooking presented few dangers. There were of course heat, flies, and mosquitoes, and the farmer's anger if stooks were badly built. There were real dangers for teamsters though, and for men working around the thresher. Crosby Johnson from Middle Stewiacke fell off a wagon—probably a runaway—in 1924 and died of his injuries.[15] Forking into the mill, with its array of whirling crooked knives, was potentially dangerous. Robert J. Stead in his queer stilted account of prairie life tells of a boy who nearly was cut to pieces in a separator:

"Walter Peters...not yet more than fifteen or sixteen, slim and straight and willing but without either the weight or the skill for a spike-pitcher...having thrust the head of his fork under the band of a sheaf so that it became caught in the cord, threw fork and all onto the feeding-table. Realizing the damage that would be done to the machinery and the shame which would engulf him for such a blunder, he lurched forward frantically for the fork...lost his balance and himself fell on the mowing sheaf! There was a chance that the carriers would stick with this extra weight but the lad was light and they swept him up toward the knives like grain for the threshing."

The hero of the story, a teen-age boy himself, saw the danger, threw himself on the great drive belt so that it came off the wheel and let the machinery stop in time. "The separator stopped like a ship upon a rock." "Mustn't take a chance like that," said an old thresherman to the young spike-pitcher who was crawling back on his load, "you'll make a sausage machine out of old Bill's straw-hasher."[16] The boy who threw himself on the big belt in Stead's tale could have been drawn up against the flywheel and crushed like an egg.

A story of such a tragedy was recounted to R. L. Yates. A teamster and a spike-pitcher got into a vicious fight. The pitcher shoved the teamster into the feeder of the big separator to be chopped up. In a display of lynch law the angry crew hanged the spike-pitcher from the blower of the mill.[17]

John Herd Thompson sums up the work life of a harvester:[18]

"Once hired, harvesters were put to work immediately. No farmer was prepared to see his men with time on their hands, and if help had been hired before the grain was ready to be cut they would be put to work 'choring,' picking stones or cutting brush until the real work of the harvest was ready to begin. Because of the danger from frost to a standing crop, grain in Western Canada was cut before it had fully ripened and allowed to reach maturity in the sheaf. The grain was cut by a horse drawn self-binding reaper, universally called a 'binder.' The binder would be driven by the farmer himself, by one of his sons, or by a permanent hired man. The harvest excursionist was assigned the back breaking, mind numbing task of 'stooking,' gathering eight or ten sheaves dropped by the reaper into a 'stook,' a pile designed to protect the grain from weather damage until it became ripe enough to thresh. Even old timers who romanticize pre-combine harvesting find it impossible to make stooking into anything but 'drudgery of the worst sort.'[19] Starting at dawn the harvesters raced to keep pace with the binder—bending, lifting and piling two sheaves at a time until it was dark. 'The hardest thing about it,' comments one excursionist, 'was the hands.' Stookers wore horsehide gloves which became soaked by the dew of the early morning and dried and cracked when the scorching Prairie sun rose higher in the sky, exposing the flesh of palms and fingers to create 'blisters as big as quarters.'[20] Feet and ankles got the same treatment. In the morning the dew 'gets into your shoes to mix with the dust...to make walking a trial by ordeal.'[21] It was impossible to roll up sleeves, whatever the temperature, or forearms would be rubbed raw from the rough straw. It was work that could break even men used to hard physical labour. Most of the British excursionists of 1928 were unemployed coal miners who had stood up to nine and ten hour days in the pits, but hundreds walked off the job in admission of defeat after a day in the harvest fields of the Canadian West.

"Once the crop was cut and stooked the work of threshing would begin in a district.[22] 'Threshing at home was a social event,' wrote an Ontarian observing his first prairie harvest, but threshing in the West was 'a serious business' conducted by 'paid mercenaries,' a business about which there was 'no romance, no sparking or skylarking...no shinnanigins while you work.'[23] Custom threshers with large outfits handled much of the crop in the West, and it was difficult for a harvest excursionist to find a job on a threshing crew. A smaller total labour force was needed for threshing than for the earlier stage of the harvest. The important members of a threshing crew—the engineer and the separator man—would stay with a crew from year to year and preference was usually given to farmers' sons or homesteaders when it came time to hire the teamsters and 'pitchers' who made up the rest of the crew.[24] Sometimes a transient could catch on, if he had some skill with horses, driving a bundle team loaded with sheaves to the farm's granary or the elevator. Men without experience looked for work as 'field pitchers,' helping drivers fork sheaves from stooks to bundle wagons. As small gas-powered threshing rigs became available during the teens and twenties, and average farm size increased, more farmers did their own threshing. This made it easier for an excursionist to keep working, since he could stay on with the boss who had originally hired him and fork the sheaves he had so laboriously stooked.

"Threshing was a less onerous task than stooking, which prompted a harvester joke to the effect that 'after the stooking "Bringing in the Sheaves" is a picnic. No wonder there's a hymn about that.' Threshing also tended to pay slightly higher wages. These two advantages were offset by two factors. The threshing day was generally longer, sometimes sixteen hours, since the machine could work by moonlight or lamplight if it had to be rushed to another farm. A stooker could collapse into his bed at the end of the day, but a thresher who handled a team had an hour added to both ends of his day by the necessity to hitch, unhitch, feed, and water his horses. If steam were the power source, threshing was also dangerous work. Each September and October newspapers reported deaths from boiler explosions and dismemberments from arms and clothing becoming tangled in grain separators. A careless or exhausted thresher could also meet death or injury by falling beneath wagons used to transport sheaves and grain. Medical care for a migrant harvester depended on the goodwill of his boss, and in most cases 'when a man meets with an injury his employer tries to get him off his hands as soon as possible,' reported James Colley. [25] At the request of farm organizations Workmens Compensation Acts in Manitoba, Saskatchewan, and Alberta were drafted to exclude farm workers from coverage. George Edwards of the United Farmers of Canada, Saskatchewan Section, admitted that this was 'a heartless way to look at it,' but like most farmers defended his organization's position on the grounds that farmers could not afford the deductions to create a compensation fund.[26] If a harvester were seriously injured on the job his only recourse was a civil suit for damages; if he were killed his family might not even learn the circumstances of his death."

People in the harvest excursion period were not as conscious of protection in the workplace and of industrial safety as they were to become late in the twentieth century. Certainly, none of the harvesters interviewed spoke of their work as being dangerous. Some men like Herb Dickeson of Taxis River "hit the harvest" five or six times during the 1920s. They were not conscious of danger; heat and discomfort were usually counterbalanced by good food and good wages on the prairie.

THE MARITIME PROVINCES were far more rural in the 1920s than they are today, and farming was much less mechanized, more labour-intensive. Were there any objections raised to the annual drain of labour to the West? Fruit farmers in the Annapolis Valley grumbled about the excursion taking away their pickers, until they discovered that West Indians could do the job faster and cheaper. Farm organizations raised objections. In 1908 the Secretary of Industries and Immigration in Halifax, A. S. Barnstead, noted that "the CPR was gathering up a lot of our men on the harvest excursion" and told farmers they should fight it.[27] But as prominent farmer H. R. Brown pointed out to G. V. Haythorne, no organized protest was ever made.

For that matter, there was also the old tradition of Maritimers going to the American lumber woods. Skilled woodsmen from the Maritimes chopped and "twitched" and teamed in most of the lumber camps from Maine to Minnesota.[28]

An Amherst man, pioneer Socialist Roscoe Fillmore, explained in his memoirs that Maritimers had an old tradition of seeking remunerative farm work outside the region:

"Bluenoses and herring chokers were in great demand in the New England States as farm labourers...men would cross the line, work hard for long hours over a six-week period...come back with enough money to tide them over the rest of the year."[29]

Roscoe Fillmore was not happy about his 1905 harvest experience:

"I worked near Regina...forty dollars a month and board...worked for a bachelor farmer. Tadpoles in the drinking water. Poor food: rice, teas, canned milk, porridge, bakers bread. The only meat was prairie chicken." [While "one former excursionist swears that he gained ten pounds during an Alberta harvest,"[30] some "others, however, talk of tough beef from 'thin old cows,' 'quarter inch deep pies,' pancakes nicknamed 'sweatpads,' and water 'so bad the only way you could drink it was hold your nose' as the only beverage provided."[31]]

Roscoe Fillmore continues:

"There was a 'caboose'...a portable bunkhouse for sleeping quarters, but some men preferred the straw stack: the caboose was noisy and smelly. One man's feet smelled so bad the others overcame him and held his feet under a pump in the freezing weather in an attempt to fight the stink. As for fieldwork both men and horses were driven home on two different occasions by millions of biting, stinging flying ants."

Fillmore and the other men cleaned out a well when wet weather stopped the harvest. They found three dead gophers in the water supply.

Roscoe Fillmore, however, went on several excursions and endured the conditions. When he took a job as mucker in the Rogers Pass for McDonnell and Gzowski, however, risking his life for seventy-five cents a day soon forced him to quit. He nearly froze to death riding the rods back to Toronto.[32]

D. J. Campbell, apparently of New Glasgow, went to the trouble in 1905 of writing a lengthy pamphlet warning young Maritimers about the discomfort, danger, and delusions associated with the excursion. Campbell, like Fillmore, may well have been an early Socialist; witness his title: *Young Nova Scotians at Manitoban Harvest: Freemen at Home, Slaves There.*

Campbell complains of the conditions he encountered in Manitoba and on the rail journey. Of the excursionists on the train, he wrote:

"The great majority are single.... The majority of the excursionists are new men...utterly inexperienced in the ways of the great outside world. The reason why so few are old hands is simply this: former excursionists as a rule were not pleased with the treatment received, and, just because a singed cat shuns fire, they prefer to stay at home, or go anywhere else, rather than risk a second trip to Manitoba."[33]

Lunches could, it seems, be obtained on the excursion train on which Campbell travelled, at prices double or triple the usual price. At stations they might pay for a dinner and have only time to eat a few bites before the train left. The farmers were penny-pinching tyrants, cutting wages at the slightest provocation, and threatening to withhold the return fare certificate if the harvester complained. Work was for sixteen hours a day pitching thirty tons of grain—far longer than in the coal mines.

The only meat available was pork, "slaughtered the preceding autumn and salted down in a barrel in which it awaited resurrection until the Nova Scotia boys came to feast on it. Now, it came forth either as salt or modified carrion.... Sugarless, and often milk-less, tea or coffee was furnished;...water could be had" but it was not drinkable. And even though the work required no training the "Manitoban tyrant" cut wages in half if job seekers admitted to having no farming experience. Good-hearted men "are temporar-ily subjected to conditions that would disgrace African slavery."[34]

Strong stuff this! Of the twenty people inter-viewed for this book who had gone on the harvest be-fore 1908, none described conditions anywhere near as dreadful as Campbell encountered. And yet a very famous western editor, social critic, and humorist also attacked the rapacity and greed of western farmers around the turn of the century:

"The hiring process went like this: You asked how much he was paying. 'Oh, twenty-five to an experi-enced hand.' Then in your innocence you would ask, 'How late do you work here?' 'Oh,' would come the careless reply, 'we unhitch at six o'clock.' What hap-pened? It is worth recalling. Up in the morning at five cleaning out the barn, feeding the horses, milking the cows and chopping a cord or two of wood, all before breakfast. Should it happen to be Monday, washday, you pack about twenty buckets of water in the house to fill the boiler. Then the breakfast and the li'l old ba-con and eggs.

"Thereafter you sally forth with your team and put in a hard day's lick. For the first week the farmer's rather sociable and communicative, getting a line on what kind of chap you are and how much you will stand for. If you are big enough to beat his head off he is likely to continue being quite sociable. If not, look out! Yes, you unhitch at six o'clock all right enough....

But it is for the horses' sake, not yours...more bacon and eggs and then—o accursed memory, the chores! All those bloody cows to milk over again, the horses to bed down and feed, wood to chop and water to fetch into the house for the morning."[35]

Eloquent thoughts from Bob Edwards, editor of the Calgary *Eye Opener*. Bob knew whereof he spoke— as a young immigrant from Edinburgh he had put in his time on prairie farms. However, he believed that things were improving. A hired man had won a wage case against a farmer—a Lethbridge magistrate had decided that the hired man on the farm was worth seventy-five dollars a month. Even the Manitoba farmers, notorious for taking advantage of their workers, would have to mend their ways.[36]

Harvesting Operations—Ground Power Combine, circa 1910.
(Courtesy Provincial Archives of Manitoba)

CHAPTER 6

In the West
More Voices from the Harvest Excursions

"**I** GOT A SCHOOL at Sedley, Saskatchewan. Most of the people were Russian or German. The children were well-behaved, could speak little English. I was supposed to live by myself in a log teacherage, a little one-room shanty with a potbellied stove in it. Not for me! I stayed in a farmhouse. Even there I got very sick. The people I stayed with sent for another teacher, Mary Gillis. She found I had a high temperature and took me to a doctor in Saskatoon. After I got better I taught in a Catholic school in Swift Current. I left the West after a year, however, trained for a nurse, and nursed for forty years in New York."

"**I** WENT TO ARCOLA, Saskatchewan, for the 1914 harvest season. I spent two days looking for work. Then a farmer hired me, drove me to his farm in a Gray-Dort touring car. My first time in a car! He had a quarter section and I was the only hired man. I got sick right away from the alkali water—got the runs. Got used to it after a while, though. They used me all right. There was lots to eat. The first day we stooked until dark, then he told me to go to the house. But it was locked up. The woman was in the barn milking cows. It was ten o'clock before I got to bed that night. Another night we worked until ten so the separator could move in the morning.

I didn't have much money the first year. In 1915 though I saved enough to go to barber school in Winnipeg. I might have stayed in the West, but I joined the army in 1916 and came back to New Brunswick after army service."

"**A** COMMERCIAL TRAVELLER in Winnipeg station told us about a farmer in Kirby who wanted men. My brother and I got a job there right away with an Ontario man—George Castle. He had settled there in 1900, lost his crop three years, then prospered. He had a full section of land, twenty-one horses, two mules, raised pigs, potatoes, beef as well as grain. Best man I ever worked for. We lived in the house like one of the family, wrote back and forth for years. When he wrote and told me his son died in the flu epidemic, I felt terrible.

One morning a mule stepped on my foot in the barn. I called it a 'Protestant bastard.' The boss said nothing to me then, but ten years later, in a letter, he said, 'Your Protestant mule just died.' He'd fire a man for swearing, George would! The nearest Catholic church was twelve miles away. He drove us there and back every Sunday. One rainy day he and the boys hauled firewood a long way to their own church, wood which they brought all the way from the mountains in the winter.

We had good threshing weather that year [1915] until late November. I came home and enlisted in the 12th Battalion."

"**I**N 1917 OUR TRAIN WENT right past Winnipeg.

Five of us went to Moose Jaw, then down the Soo Line to Drinkwater. A farmer named Braun hired us. We slept on sheaves in the barn the first night and rolled around all night. Meals were okay, though there were no afternoon lunches. Braun's German wife caught pigeons and cooked them for our meals. Braun himself had poor gear, a lot of breakdowns. Used to get drunk on weekends to forget his troubles. But he used us all right.

We'd been warned about alkali water, so we had extract of wild strawberry to sort of neutralize it. When we were on the move with the thresher we would sometimes have only stream water to drink. It wasn't too bad after we strained it through cheesecloth to get the maggots and crawlers out of it.

Just the same, I would have stayed in the West, but my buddy was determined to go home. See now, plenty of women stayed in the West, taught a year or two, then got married. It was easy to catch a man out there. Not many harvesters stayed to farm, anyway. But see now, if you were looking to homestead, you'd go out in the spring, to get set for those awful winters. Now I did save some money. I went out with thirty-one dollars, went home with sixty in my pocket after buying clothes in Winnipeg. I went into the bank, became a manager after a while."

"**GERMANS WERE THE BEST FARMERS** to work for, English the worst. In '21 I got a job firing—feeding straw into the Cock o' the North steam engine's firebox all day long. The engineer was from the Miramichi too, he had stationary engineer's papers. He got fifteen dollars a day, I got ten—far better than field work. I went back to the same place every year for five years. Saved seven or eight hundred dollars each year. Back home it was two dollars a day and feed yourself.

We never worked Sunday, though you could get a permit from the Mounties to do so. Across the line, American outfits threshed every Sunday. They had no boiler inspection either, like we did.

We were often paid with grain cheques; no problem cashing them. Never any trouble getting our money.

If you were a Maritimer, you were just about sure of getting a job in the West!"

"**I WORKED FOR MY UNCLE** on a Saskatchewan farm. Four dollars for stooking, six for threshing. We stacked fifteen days without rain, following two eight-foot Massey Harris binders. When hauling to the thresher we always left one load in the field for the morning. We were up at daylight, in the field at six, had a big lunch at eleven, a lunch in the field at three P.M. We took turns eating lunch so no time was lost. We worked until dark, or seven. Snow and sleet put an end to threshing on October 20."

"**F**ROM **WINNIPEG WE TOOK A TRAIN** to Moose Jaw, then went south to Briercrest. I worked with two wheat farmers, each with a full section—240 acres. Very friendly people around there. They heard us sing and soon had us in the church choir. I was invited to their homes and to local affairs. They wanted us to stay all winter, offered me a job at the rink. But I had a girl back home in North Sydney, though she didn't know it then. I went out again to the West in '24—worked in Briercrest again. Bumper crop of wheat. We were up at 4 A.M., feed the horses and brush them, clean the stable, then harness up. Then we would have breakfast, water the horses and hitch them to a rack wagon. We'd follow the stook loader that filled our racks with sheaves. Then up to the Rumley separator, a rack on each side and pitch the sheaves into the feeder. The straw and chaff blew out of a big funnel, while the wheat poured into a wheat wagon to be taken to the elevator or stored in bins on the farm.

One bad thing about that country: the water was poison to Easterners. Just like drinking Epsom salts. The work was okay once you got used to pitching sheaves all day and the blisters on your hands broke and your hands got as tough as shoe leather.

In 1925 four of us worked near Yorkton, then Rosetown. We finished up in November with a couple of hundred dollars each in our money belts. We hoboed through to British Columbia, stayed the winter, then worked our way back east. The others went to Montreal or Toronto. I went to Boston for a while, went home and sang my way into my North Sydney girl's heart. We eloped, got married in Glace Bay, and went to the States. I've worked near forty years here, first with RCA Victor, then with Dictograph of Jamaica, New York. Wife and I celebrate our fiftieth this year [1977]."

"**O**UTSIDE OF WINNIPEG I STOPPED a northbound train, using a burning newspaper as a flare. We got off at Solsgirth and found jobs there. I was with an English family—Fentons—that had farmed in the United States. Too many Germans where they were, so they moved to Manitoba.

They used me well, good meals and everything. My friend who went to a nearby farm got so sick on the alkali water that he had to quit. He got money from his brother, a bank manager in Winnipeg, to go home to New Brunswick.

I refused to stook barley. The awns made me so sore and itchy I couldn't sleep at night. I threatened to quit and Fenton put me back doing oats and wheat. There was a make-and-break gas engine running the separator which Fenton and two other men owned. I stayed until snow and cold came in late October. Shot a lot of ducks.

On the way home I pinned my money to my undershirt and foiled some pickpockets on the train. I joined the artillery when war broke out and was soon driving mules in France. After that I sold insurance in Fredericton."

"**I HAD THE PROMISE OF A SCHOOL** before going out—my aunt in Saskatchewan had arranged that. I was to replace a girl from Ontario who got lonesome and quit. A one-room school I had with fifty pupils, mostly German and Scandinavian. Many big teenage boys came in late in the term, after harvest was over. Scandinavian children were bright and very musical. Four years I taught in that school. It stayed open in winter while I was there, though some schools were forced to close in severe winter weather. In fact my school closed for winter the year after I left. What was the salary? One thousand dollars a year, compared to three thirty-seven in New Brunswick."

"**I WORKED TWO YEARS** at Settere, then in '22 I went to a place south of Regina. Always got paid when I asked for it—the farmer would get a man to haul grain to the elevator so he'd have money to pay us. One year the snow came and stopped threshing, the farmer had to finish in the spring. I worked mostly for

English farmers; they used me all right. They had great gardens. Their meat was mostly provided through a beef ring: a bunch of farmers would take turns killing a beef and the meat would be divided up. There was no refrigeration to keep it long. There was no electricity, but they had windmills to pump water.

We went into town a little. All the towns were the same: a garage and livery stable, a Chinese restaurant, maybe a theatre or a bank.

One year I got to the farm a week too early for harvest. Worked for a week ploughing and fencing, just for my board."

"I CAME BACK from my first excursion with over two hundred dollars. I worked for my brother-in-law. I got eight dollars a day at other farms using my in-law's team and a bundle wagon at threshing time. I bought a piece of land on homestead rights, stayed a few years. The first three years I leased my land to a farmer and worked for another farmer near North Battleford. Then the drought hit in '29, I didn't get a good crop for five years. Finally I sold out to my brother-in-law and went home to Pictou County."

"I WORKED FIRST for French farmers at Ponteix, Saskatchewan. A poor year there—very wet. Then I went north, worked with a farmer from Ontario. There were so many harvesters in '24 that the farmers beat us down to three dollars for stooking, four fifty for threshing. I ate like a starved wolf—I was only eighteen. That big lunch in the afternoon just put an edge on my appetite. In August we broke ice on the water barrels to get a drink in the morning.

Up there was a terrible place for snakes. They came out of the stony creek bottoms, were under sheaves when we were stooking. Some were poison, I guess, but I never heard of anyone being bitten."

"**I** WORKED NEAR WEYBURN for an American farmer—an immigrant, that is. Name was John Jacobson. He often said he wished he had stayed in the States. I got there too late for stooking. I slept in a bunkhouse on wheels. It and the cookshack were pulled from one farm to another by horses when the threshing outfit moved. I saved all I earned. I saw a poor young fellow who was robbed of every cent he had by a pickpocket in Winnipeg. We had to help him."

"**W**E WERE BROKE AND HUNGRY getting into Winnipeg. Bought a bag of candy for thirty-five cents to stave off starvation. Somebody told us there were jobs at Maryfield, Saskatchewan. There we slept in the station a night with a whole lot of bohunks who all carried big knives. Next morning they made huge baloney sandwiches. Two of my buddies went off with a Swedish farmer in a buckboard wagon. Another fellow and I were hired by a Scotchman. He bought us a steak dinner in a Chinese restaurant for a quarter— yes, twenty-five cents each—and drove us to the farm in a T Model Ford, the back seat full of binder twine. Four dollars a day he offered for stooking. At the end of the season he paid us five dollars a day—said we were the best men he ever had. I sent a draft for a hundred sixty-five dollars home. Good farmer, that Scotchman! He had cattle, pigs, monstrous potatoes, fine big horses on his place, a diesel engine on the thresher, and a big Case tractor."

"**I** GOT MY JOB through Ernie Cotton, a P. E. Islander who lived near me in Trenton. He had worked at this farmer's— Brakewell's—before, and I got hired right on when I mentioned him. Ernie stayed there all winter once, and they sure liked him. But it was a bad year when I was there—rain or trying to rain for six weeks. We pitched horseshoes, milked cows, hauled rocks for a foundation. He paid us three dollars a day for that kind of work—we didn't expect to get any pay until threshing began. He was a great guy. American, he was.

I shot no ducks, but got two great big jack rabbits one day. However, Brakewell's Polish wife wouldn't cook them. Got no liquor there—he was a temperance man. Saw no booze except a bottle of Canadian Club I bought in Winnipeg. Could have used some beer—the water at Brakewell's was terrible. It would rust a tin can overnight!

He had a small house and a fine big barn, a gas tractor and a twenty-eight-inch separator. Mostly wheat and oats on that farm, a little barley and flax. Flax was terrible stuff to handle.**"**

"I HAD BEEN OUT ON THE HARVEST a couple of times, and eventually homesteaded in northern Saskatchewan, in the Birch Hills. There was a settlement there of Nova Scotians. Some were from Pictou County, some from Antigonish, and a few from Cape Breton to add zest to the thing. My father and mother went out to visit them. When my father saw the north country, a new country, a land of woods and water, lush with pea vines waist-high, soil so rich all you needed to do was fluff it up a little, drop a seed in and jump back! He had rassled with the stony soil of Barney's River all his life, now he said the Northwest was the place for us to go. He went out and settled in Birch Hills.

I went out on the harvest and landed in the

south—a flat country, little towns, grain elevators, you could see for forty miles. No trees. It made me lonely. I longed for a cat spruce!

Up where my father homesteaded on a fractional half section, the land was teeming with game. Myriads of ducks, flying up out of them sloughs, the water streaming off their wings sounded like heavy rain!

I went out in the fall of '26, homesteaded on two hundred and two acres of government land with Father. Thirty-seven hundred dollars he paid for it. Some land broke but no houses. The neighbours helped. We all worked like dogs and put up buildings.

At that time Saskatchewan had the highest per capita farm income of any province in Canada—one thousand six hundred dollars per farm. By 1931 it was the lowest in Canada, a per capita income of sixty-six dollars. By 1936 the farmers of Saskatchewan were destitute.

We couldn't see that coming, of course. We used all horses—tractors would bog down in that country where we were. Horses were cheap, thirty-five or forty dollars, although they often got a sort of swamp fever that killed them. Had to get machinery too. Then the crash came in '29. We knew little about it—it seemed as remote as a war in the Holy Land. We had a battery radio. Mostly there was just squeaks and sputters on it, but you could grasp a word now and again. Electric power? No! Only power we had was the shotgun. We did have the telephone, though; and we weren't bothered by hail—it followed hills to the north and south.

1930 was the best crop we ever grew—seventeen hundred and some bushels of wheat. Number One wheat was then one dollar twenty-five cents a bushel in 1928 and 1929. In 1930 our wheat wasn't quite good enough for Number One, but it was good Number

A harvest excursion crew from Nova Scotia and Ontario threshing wheat at Vanguard, Saskatchewan, 1928. From left to right: brothers Aubrey and Fred Chapman from Stellarton, Nova Scotia; owners Frank Shepherd and Frank Woods, and Bobbie Burns and Joe Fanning from Ontario. The threshing machine, a 21-inch Wood Brothers product, could thresh approximately 1,000 bushels of wheat a day. *(Courtesy of Fred Chapman, Stellarton, N.S.)*

A harvest excursion crew from Nova Scotia, Ontario and Montana, threshing wheat for Flett Wall at Aneroid, Saskatchewan, 1928. The thresher, one of the largest in existence, had a 44-inch cylinder which could thresh 2,500 bushels of wheat a day. Straw was used to generate steam for the large steam tractor. *(Courtesy of Fred Chapman, Stellarton, N.S.)*

Ronald Parker and two friends— all from Berwick, Nova Scotia, 1926. *(Courtesy of Jack Kyte, New Glasgow, N.S.)*

Two—two years before we would have got one dollar twenty cents for it. In 1930 we got eighteen cents a bushel. That was the sad sombre story of the '30s in the West. It struck us like a bolt of lightning, with no warning at all.

There was no starvation where we were. But down in the south, toward Regina, the Depression was accompanied by drought, rust, hail, grasshoppers, and sawfly! Up in Birch Hills we could grow food to feed ourselves. Down in the prairie they could not.

There was no relief, no welfare, no old age pensions. There was R. B. Bennett, Premier in Ottawa, brought up with a silver spoon in his mouth, no sympathy or understanding of ordinary people's problems.

Well, in 1930 we had to sell one thousand bushels of wheat just to pay the threshing bill. That wasn't enough to settle it, so we had to sell a cow too.

I married a woman from Nova Scotia in the West. We stuck it out through the '30s, then came back with our family by train to Nova Scotia, just when things were starting to get better. Sold all the stock and machinery. I sat in the house and cried when an auctioneer was selling my horses. Why did we come back then? I'll tell you. Willa and I—she was a teacher— were determined to get our children educated. And we didn't think they would get an education in the West. We came back to Pictou County. I owned my father's house there. Worked in the steel works during the war, and did some auctioneering and the family got a good education."

"WE REACHED WINNIPEG at midnight. Not in the CPR station! Oh no! Us harvesters were herded into long sheds near the station. That's where the hiring agents were. Now the Nova Scotians paid the agents no heed at all. They knew where they were going. 'Don't bother with those birds!' they said. 'They can't guarantee a job! Go to any little town and you'll get work!' Well, my buddy did that, but I had no intention of sweating my guts out on the harvest. I stayed with my sister, who was married to a CPR fireman in Winnipeg. Got a brakeman job on the CP. Not much work though—there were three hundred brakemen on the spare board in Winnipeg station. I came back to New Brunswick and got a job on the Canadian Government Railways."

"**R**AY AND I GOT TO WINNIPEG early, stayed in a hotel in Milestone, Saskatchewan, until the grain was ready. The girl on the desk in the hotel was a sister to Danny 'Mikkle' MacDonald—I had worked with him in the Six Foot mine.

After the harvest began I worked with an American—Ross Cunningham. Place was okay. We had stuff to put in the alkali water so it didn't ream the guts out of us. The next year I worked for a German—Schoefler—at Last Mountain. Great fellow to work for. I made a batch of beer for him and the threshing went fast that day!

I saved a little each trip. I had no notion of staying in the West though—heard the winters were rough."

"**F**ROM WINNIPEG WE WENT right to Calgary. Two policemen came up to us at the station, gave us tickets to a place two hundred miles away on the Goose Lake Line. Got hired by Belgian farmers. Nice people, good food, good spring water. I stayed until the fall—they cried when I left. I had an uncle a minister in Calgary. Stayed with him a while, then went home.

I fished lobsters next spring, then a neighbour coaxed me to go on the harvest. He'd never been out west and he was after a girl who had run out on him. He'd heard she was in Edmonton. I sold the fishing gear—the boat was old anyway—and we went on a late excursion.

I went back to the Belgians, but they had already hired a man. However, the boss of the B/A Oil Company was a sort of hiring agent. He got me on with an Ontario farmer, 'Toothpick Dan' Sutherland. Quite a schemer was Dan. The food was slack enough until I 'made up' to his starched and powdered daughter. Great eats then! 'Toothpick Dan' told me of a farm for lease—eight hundred acres—north of there. The owner—Robinson—had a Swedish farm manager who was always plastered. Donald Cameron and I took the farm—four hundred acres—on the halves with Robinson.

We had bad luck—were hailed out for three years straight. I saw hail a foot thick on the road in August. You couldn't get the car through it without chains. Crops were as flat as if harrowed. Time to get out, says I. My hail insurance came through. The wife and I headed east in November with three hundred and thirty dollars. Twenty-nine dollars left when we reached Pictou County."

"**W**E TOOK A CHANCE and went up the Biggar line. A man wearing a big hat at the station said, 'You're looking for work, eh?' We stooked there until October, finished the job, then went to the employment office in Edmonton. They sent us to St. Albert. French farmers, poor food, but we stayed a month. Wood-burning steam tractors for threshing.

In 1928 we went to a big outfit on Bow Island, Alberta. Twelve teams hauling in. There were lumber-jacks from the coast working there, Swedes, Swiss, even a taxi driver from Winnipeg. We slept on straw in a big wall tent—took only our boots off at night. Lanterns for light and warmth. Alkali water—yeah, I could drink it, but you could not shave with it—just would not lather.

I counted once four hundred sheaves of wheat on an eight-by-sixteen wagon. I saw a combine working that year, sixteen-foot cut, twelve horses pulled it. I drove a four-horse team hauling one hundred and forty bushels of grain to the elevator, hauled four tons of coal on the return trip.**"**

"WE SLEPT IN THE STATION at Winnipeg the first night—had no money left. Then my cousin phoned a fellow whose farm he had worked on before and he gave us a job. Four dollars for stooking, five for threshing. Good food. Stayed in a bunkhouse, then in a bunkcar when threshing. Gas tractor. Worked in Davidson, Saskatchewan, for an Englishman named Hume. Used us good.

Alkali water didn't bother me, but my cousin had a serious time with it for a whole week. Didn't save much money, went to town nearly every weekend. Big snowstorm in October put an end to threshing and we came home.

In 1927 we went CPR, went to Vanguard, Saskatchewan. Got a dollar more that year. Frank Shepherd from Wisconsin was the farmer, used us great. I slept in a homesteader's shack, ate in the house. Went out to Alberta, near Lethbridge. We had trouble getting our money there—that was the only time that happened. Mounties helped us get our money—they were great to help you anyway.

I had no desire to spend the rest of my life out there—too many blizzards for me."

"COAL MINERS WERE in great demand on the harvest because they were used to keeping their heads down all day loading coal with a pan shovel, and conditions in harvest fields were just as exacting. We worked near Swift Current, then went to work near Carberry for North Dakota Swedes. Slept in a granary, where the mice were so bad we bailed out one night and slept in a stook wagon. First a cow came rubbing herself against the wagon, then a wind came up and blew our blankets away. So Leroy and I went to a place near Success run by a Scotchman, Donald Murchie. A Norwegian woman cooked for us and her two boys worked with us. We'd go to town on Saturday, Leroy and I and Murchie riding in a Concord wagon while the boys rode horseback. One Saturday Murchie and the boys got stoned. We put them in the wagon and rode horseback to the farm. My horse was wild—he galloped the whole four miles to the farm!

There was a Baldridge family, three brothers from England, and a Phillips man that had built homes, four of them on close corners of a section. It made a little community near Success. We worked there a while. I remember late in October one year I was caught in a blinding snowstorm while hauling the last load of wheat that day. Couldn't see a thing. I tied the horses and got under the wagon. I was scared! There came a lull in the storm, I heard a door slam, then Reg Baldridge's voice. I untied the horses and they took me to the barn. I was some glad to get there!

We made a lot of friends in Success. One Saturday Leroy Lawley and I were in town; we met a young fellow from New Brunswick with his arm in a sling. He knew us, as he had come out on the train with us. He had an infected hand from the pitchfork. He told us a gang of toughs came in every night picking on him since he'd been hurt. 'Here they come now!' he says. They looked kind of hostile. Now both Leroy and I had done a little boxing. Leroy pasted the ringleader, who was the elevator man's son, and the rest took off. We thought the townspeople would be down on us, but they said we'd done them a favour.

In 1925 I was in Vancouver on a government job, when I got the urge to go back to the Prairies. Went on a harvest train through the Rockies to Oyen on the Goose Lake line. A Jewish man named Cooper ran a beer parlour there, a great place for harvesters from the West Coast to gather on Saturday night. In 1926 I went to Virden Valley, worked with a Czech family. It turned out that they had lived in Caledonia—Glace Bay—for a while before coming west, and knew my people.

I worked in the coal mines in Drumheller. Lots of Easterners there, from Springhill and Cape Breton. I did a bit of boxing. I won the Welterweight Championship of Western Canada by KO'ing Tommy Rogers in the fourth round, in 1925. He was an Englishman who had started his boxing career in Cambridge University.

When the Depression struck I came back to Nova Scotia, worked as a lineman."

"**W**E WENT RIGHT FROM WINNIPEG to Regina, were hired right at the station. Just two questions the farmer asked: 'Can you handle horses? Can you stook grain?' If you said 'yes' to both you were hired. We worked for a Scotchman—Bill Dickie. He liked Nova Scotians, said they weren't scared of work.

Great setup: he had a whole section [640 acres], good gear and buildings. Ten workers slept in a bunkhouse. German cooks, and they were first rate. I never ate better in my life. A cook would be out in the field at ten thirty in the morning with a truckload of sandwiches and tea. Fine big horses he had. Some would go nineteen hundredweight. Lord! They were like elephants—you could hardly reach the tops of their necks to put the hames over. Had his own separator, trucks and tractors.

I had a driving licence, used to drive the crew into town Saturday. We never worked Sundays, though some crews did. All the rest of our crew were from Ontario. Us two men from Nova Scotia were the only Christians. But I never was in church or had a bath all the time I was there. For twenty-six days we had no rain, then it rained for a week. Great crop that year. I saved four hundred dollars. Pay was good: six dollars for stook, seven for thresh. I had a hundred bucks on me in a moneybelt, sent the rest home through the bank.

We went back to Dickie's in '27. There were Mounties on the train from Quebec on, so there was no raiding that year. Crop was not as good. I ploughed with a three-furrow plough—it was like ploughing ashes! We wrote to him in '28, but he had a combine and didn't need us. He wanted me to come anyhow and stay there all winter. He had all those horses and five hundred head of cattle to look after. 'Hell, no!' says I, 'stay alone in that ungodly cold with nothing to listen to but coyotes howling? Not me!' In '27 it was terrible cold dry weather the last week we threshed. We hauled grain to the separator with bobsleighs.

I went to Detroit, worked in a factory until the '31 crash, then got on the lake boats. Good money—six dollars and five cents a day, fifteen dollars for Sunday work. In '37 came back to Lakevale and drove the mail. Came home to Mabou finally."

"FOUR OF US WENT STOOKING for a farmer near Vanguard, the other four went on to Alberta. My farmer's name was Sparling. He had come up from Indiana with his family when just a child. He had a smallish gas rig, threshed just a few farms. When he was done we got on a big steam threshing rig run by a Norwegian. Cook cars, bunk cars, the whole bit. Four dollars a day we got for stooking, six for threshing. Twelve hours a day. It was two dollars a day then in the pulp woods back in New Brunswick.

Never saw any snakes where we worked, no. But one day I was harrowing summer fallow before the grain was ready. I was set on by swarms of flying ants. They bit me bad.

We started walking the six miles to town one night. A Quebec threshing crew, mostly Frenchmen, picked us up and took us to town. On the way back we tried to get on with them. The driver—an English guy—was drunk, galloped the horses and wouldn't let us get on the wagon. But the Frenchmen made him stop and take us on."

"FIVE OF US WORKED for a McLaughlin man near Milestone, Saskatchewan. Slept in the granary. He had a coal-fired steam thresher. We couldn't drink the well water—awful stuff. They got ice water for us somewhere. Five dollars a day, and no trouble getting paid.

I went out again on the CPR train in '26. Worked near Kinistino for Jack Jackson. His wife was a Gordon from Piedmont.

Didn't save much money either year."

"**D**AN CHISHOLM AND I WORKED for George Ray, an Ontario man, near Pilot Mound, Manitoba. We were well fed and housed—it was a good place to work. We stayed ploughing for him until November, until our excursion tickets had nearly expired, then went home.

I came out in 1912, worked on the Connaught Tunnel job for two years. Lots of Maritimers in the West then."

"**I**N '26 NORM MACLELLAN AND I worked near Claresholm, Alberta. I stayed until November ploughing for a MacKenzie man—three-furrow plough pulled by seven horses. Then I ran a ranch for three weeks for a man I'd worked for before—George Barr—while he was in hospital.

Alkali water did not bother me. Almost killed Norman, though. We went through the mountains to British Columbia late in the fall. Couldn't buy a job there. I went to Detroit for a while, then came back to Nova Scotia—my father got hurt in the pit."

"**W**HEN WE GOT TO WINNIPEG my buddy and I looked at a map and decided to take the Soo Line train to Assiniboine. At the station there we saw a man with a bag full of kittens, went up and asked for a job. He was Frank Scobie from Kalamazoo, Michigan. He farmed four hundred acres of wheat. We worked for him for two seasons. In '20 we were too early for grain, so we spent thirteen days digging a cellar for his new house. He paid us three dollars a day for that. We lived in a rough bunkhouse. Flies everywhere— there were no screens. Hundreds of hens around the place. We ate a lot of corn and tomatoes. Scobie was a good man to work for in spite of the flies. I saved over three hundred dollars. The snow came early in '22 and we went home—should have gone to British Columbia.

I worked a while one year for an Adams man near Assiniboine. He was from Los Angeles—he had come all the way up from there by ox wagon. Good man to work for. He was sort of crippled.

I drank cold milk at noon to avoid the alkali water. Scobie kept a creamer of milk down the well. I went to the States for a while, then came back to work as a lineman for Nova Scotia Light and Power Company."

"WE WENT RIGHT ON TO MOOSE JAW and got hired right away. Cradock, an Englishman, was the farmer. He fed well and used us all right. Good drinking water too, from a neighbour's drilled well. We got three fifty for stooking, five dollars for threshing. He had a stook loader that saved pitching on. He owned the separator himself, but a neighbour owned the Rumley steamer that made the thresher go. There was one problem—we got lousy in the bunkhouse and had to douse the crawlers with Creolin.

In September a big snowstorm put an end to threshing. I came back to the Annapolis Valley. I had saved some of my earnings on the harvest. Took up the bricklaying trade and worked at it all over eastern North America."

"JOHN REDFORD WAS THE NAME of the farmer where I worked, near Landis, Saskatchewan. Food was okay, though I had to sleep on straw in the barn. I wanted to go to town to dances, but had no money at all until I was paid off. Four dollars a day from four in the morning until eight at night.

Lord, I was lonesome! It was my first time away from home. I cried with happiness at Sylvan Valley when I could see the lights of Antigonish from the train. I worked at different jobs, then became a policeman for most of my life.

Looking back, I'd say the harvest excursion was the worst trip I ever had!"

"**T**WO FRIENDS AND I WENT to Saskatoon and were hired. I took a taxi to a farm near Watrous. The farmer was a foreigner of some kind. He had a little English, his wife and kids had none. I was working alone trying to stook one hundred fifty acres that he had cut. He wanted me to work Sunday; I refused and quit.

I tried to reach the farm where my buddies were working, but was lost all night on the prairie. Monday I went back to the foreigner's farm. He hired more stookers and I stayed on. I went spike-pitching when threshing started. One fearful windy day they had to keep shifting the mill around; all I got was a bellyful and lungs full of dust. I drank strong rye whiskey and water, was terrible sick that night. But next day I was okay!

I managed to get a jug of good water and kept it hidden. I saw fellows get awful sick on the alkali water.

Harvest was nearly over when my brother wrote wanting me to go home. At the station the agent, a man from Ontario, fed me and stopped the midnight train so I could get on it. He warned me not to 'change money' with crooks on the train and to watch for pickpockets. I put my money in my shoes and kept 'em on my feet at night, laces tied in a hard knot. A man from Sydney sitting near me kicked a pickpocket through the end door when he tried to get his money."

"**I** WORKED TWO OR THREE PLACES. Worked for an Olson man, thirty miles out of Moose Jaw. They were musical people and used to have us in singsongs around the piano on weekends or rainy evenings. I got in trouble there, though. One day some mail came for me. I got another man to feed the mill while I was reading my mail. He let a fork go into the feeder and wrecked the mill. I was blamed and got the heave-ho.

That wasn't the only time I was fired—another place I lost my watch when stooking. I could after that only guess at the time by looking at the shadow on the stubble. I came in too early at noon one day and the boss gave me my walking ticket. In the evening you couldn't guess wrong—you started home as soon as the sun began to hit the horizon. If you waited, it was black dark all of a sudden, just as though somebody had pulled down a blind, and you were lost on the prairie.

My last boss, a drunk, fired me because I refused to try to harness a wild, kicky team. I walked fifteen miles into Moose Jaw, went through to Vancouver on the train, down to the States, then back to Glencoe in Nova Scotia, in the East River Valley. I've farmed and logged here ever since—seventy years ago that was, in 1905. Shot a lot of moose since then too, and b'iled a lot of maple syrup."

"**I** WORKED FOR OLSON'S in Saskatchewan. Good place. After the harvest I went to California with singer Wilf Carter and three other fellows in an old car. We picked fruit in the San Joaquin Valley in southern California, then back home to Sackville through the States."

"**I** WENT ON PAST WINNIPEG to Lethbridge with a dozen or so other Cape Breton men. We were too early for the harvest there. It was awful wet. I had twenty dollars and we stayed in a rooming house. Finally we went to a slave market [employment agency] where we saw a sign: 'Three harvesters wanted.' One of us could harness a horse so we got the job, building grade for a railroad near Cardston.

I drove a dump cart, for which I got two dollars a day and board. After six weeks the weather broke. Two of us drew our time and went into Cardston. Right quick a farmer hired us for a sixteen bundle-rack outfit. Eight dollars a day I earned for twenty-five days. Great! Good grub, and we could get an advance from the boss farmer to go to Lethbridge if it was too wet to thresh.

After harvest I went to Coalhurst. I had Nova Scotia miner's papers—you didn't need papers in Alberta mines then. The pit boss had been a pit boss in Number 12 mine in New Waterford. I got a good job right quick. Better pay than back home in the mines. For a few years I worked on farms in the spring, on harvest in summer, hoboed around. I went to British Columbia in '32. Got a job in Stanley Park; the hiring boss was from Glace Bay. I finally went back east, built wharves in Saint John, graded apples in the Valley for two dollars a day, then went back to the pit."

"**A**N EMPLOYMENT AGENCY in Saskatoon got jobs for us. I worked near Leney for an Ontario farmer, a real driver of men. But he had a nice English wife who washed our clothes for us. I went off every few days with a team and a ninety-gallon molasses puncheon for drinking water.

After a while I went to work for a German, a good man to work for. I saved a wild team for him once: they stampeded when the mill whistle blew. I caught the reins and held on though they dragged me quite a piece. A very heavy crop, enough to plug the mill at times.

I went into town one Saturday, saw no women on the streets. But when I went into a store there were ten women in it. Guess they were scared to go on the street while harvesters were around. I got booze in a speakeasy for twenty-five cents a shot.

We had a great cook at the German's place. She was as cross as a grizzly bear. But she was trying to learn to play the fiddle. A fellow from Quebec and I would get in the kitchen with her after supper. One of us would raid the pantry while the other taught her fiddle tunes. Great fun!

One man I was with threshed ten sections. So much wheat he had to pile it on the ground. He wanted me to stay all winter hauling grain for thirty-five dollars a month and board. But I didn't want to stay in the West. Everything was spread out too far, it made you feel queer and lonesome and small.

At one place I had to wait around for my wages all day while the farmer was collecting from fellows he had threshed for. When he paid me off he said, 'Come back next year! There's a job here for you!'"

"**A GERMAN FELLOW** from Scotsburn and I were hired on at Nutana, out of Saskatoon. A German farmer. Well treated and fed. We stooked three weeks, threshed for five. I hardly ever went to town, saved over one hundred dollars. Two men tried to fleece us out of our money in Montreal Station en route home, but the police looked after them. I had no desire to stay in the West, though I liked it well enough. My brother went out on the harvest in '19 and stayed out afterward, working on the extra gang on the railroad. Then he took an engineering degree at the University of Saskatchewan and went to Boston to work as an engineer."

"IN HIGH RIVER I stooked one week for Fred Knupp, an Ontario farmer. Went threshing after that with a Von Winkle man. He had a Rumley tractor, a 40/60 separator. On the crew with me there were two High River men and a Memramcook Frenchman, and the rest were hoboes. I had a great team of horses that year. But rain and snow hit in only eight days after threshing began, so I didn't do well. In '26 I worked near Colfax. A good year, I saved two hundred dollars. Never had any trouble getting money.

I farmed and worked at different jobs after coming home to Shepody."

"WE WORKED NEAR ARDATH in '22. A Stewiacke girl there helped get jobs for us. The farmer was Herb Brooks from Ontario. No complaints from us about food or pay. The bad water bothered me some. One man got sick from it right upon the load, had no time to get off, and he had to crap right into the load of sheaves. I often wonder how that load graded! There were eight of us spike-pitching, four Canadians and four Russians. We had a sort of competition. We crossed each others' lines, pulled kingpins out of wagons, threw a load of spiny Russian thistles on one Russian who went to sleep. All in fun. Farmer took us to church on Sunday. I stayed to plough after the harvest. I rode a big plough pulled by six horses. The farmer said there was no need to plough straight, just keep in the same general direction! I drove a Massey-Harris binder pulled by four big Percheron horses. It was a mile down each side of the field, and the bundle-carrier kicked out six sheaves at a time. I saved five hundred dollars that year.

In '25 I worked fourteen miles from Assiniboine. Slept on an iron bed in the granary. The door was open a crack and I could see the stars. For some reason I got terrible homesick. I worked for a Scotch farmer—a great man for big Clyde horses. The rain came one year and the black gumbo soil built up on their hooves bigger than a basketball. Even hens would get stuck in the mud and have to be dug out.

I liked the West. People were kind, and they had a different outlook on life out there—bigger ideas, more ambitious and willing to take a chance. In '25 I went to town at freeze-up, got a job in a flour mill. After the mill closed—at Christmas—I got a job in the rink. Worked for an undertaker for a time, and later ran a creamery. I married a Western girl. The first time I saw her she was on a binder, driving six horses.

In 1929 things were getting rough. I was going to go home to farm near Stewiacke, but a friend steered me into working for Canada Packers in Antigonish."

"**I WORKED FOR DOUKHOBORS** for a while. Good people to work for, although I was a while getting used to the grub—roast goose, vegetable soup, loads of garlic. And they were always eating Doukhobor peanuts—sunflower seeds—and spitting out shells. I worked at the printing trade in Winnipeg a winter, then went on harvest in the summer. Worked for a retired North West Mounted Police officer one summer. I spent twelve years in the West, mostly teaming up north. We hauled ore forty-six miles from Flin Flon to load scows. I drove a 'school bus' sleigh one winter. Met only one other Pictou County man up north—a McRae from Toney River who was selling liquor in a Prince Albert hotel.

Now I tell you! Westerners have different ideas. They don't like the 'garrison mentality,' the class consciousness of many Nova Scotian people. Out west what counted was what you could do, not who you were.

The mayor of Saskatoon, a doctor from Nova Scotia, never learned that. He was too high-toned and important to let a friend of mine into his car to visit his sick wife in hospital. The next summer he came wanting my friend to pull his car out where it was stuck in deep sand. My friend told him he could stay stuck until he and the car would rot!

I left the West in '29. I was needed at home."

"STANLEY PENNINGTON, an Englishman who came to Canada in 1905, was at the station in Unity looking for men when we got off the train there. Fine place to work, but he had some wild horses. One team took off one day, ran right through a fence and over a bank into a deep slough where they drowned. And the drinking water was awful—just like soapsuds when it got a little warm, though the wells were two hundred feet deep. I went back there in '21. The next year I worked in Manitoba for a farmer from Ontario. Never went to town, saved some money. Wouldn't stay out in the prairie—too cold in winter. I farmed here in Pictou County and ran a sawmill."

"BEFORE LEAVING NEW BRUNSWICK we got

the name of a Swedish farmer outside of Saskatoon from a neighbour—Vern Noble—who had worked for him. We went there and tried to get a job on our own. The Swede said the grain was not ready. 'Vern Noble sent us!' we said, and he hired us right away. Name was Karlson. Splendid place to work. He had thirty-five horses and four binders working one and a quarter sections. We had to change all the teams at noon so the beasts would not get too tired in the heat. All coal stoves for cooking and heating—they had no electricity. There were eight children in the family and they had built three houses: one for the parents and girls, one for the boys and one for the hired men. They had a beef ring with neighbours for meat—kept the meat in a well-screened building. It kept well in the dry climate. The farmer said he grew wheat for fifteen cents a bushel and got a dollar sixty-six at the pool elevator.

At first we had to clean stables and look after the horses on Sunday. But one day we harnessed a team for one of his boys—who slept in, I guess—so he wouldn't be late, and we didn't have to do any more Sunday work. They had a half-tame coyote they had caught as a pup. You couldn't lay hands on the thing. Poultry was never safe from it.

In those days, back in the Maritimes, people had got to thinking that if you hadn't been on the harvest you hadn't been anywhere."

"**A** FARMER DROVE US to his place near Shaunavon in a Model T Ford. When we started stooking the high stubble about ruined my shoes—I should have had boots on. Water didn't bother me—I had lime juice to put in it. Saved some money.

Not knowing what he was doing, the farmer hired a Wobbly [a militant union man, member of the Indus-

trial Workers of the World] as a field pitcher. He tried
to get me to slow down. I told him to go to hell. Somebody must have squealed to the boss—the Wobbly was
soon gone.

I didn't like the West—was damn glad to get
home.**"**

"HARD **TO GET A RUN** on the railroad in the
Maritimes—the spare board was full. My brother and
I worked at Colfax for a man from Ontario who went
west before the Northwest Rebellion. He retired about
1920 and let his sons take over. Then he bought a
quarter section at a Colfax tax sale and put buildings
on it. Thunder and lightning and snow came in late
September. Wheat and barley were finished, but we
had to stack oats to be threshed in spring.

My brother and I went through the mountains to
Kamloops after the harvest. Couldn't get a job at a
lumber camp near Lytton—the company was out of
business. We got tired on the long walk back to Lytton, were getting lost. I made the secret sign of the
Brotherhood of Locomotive Engineers to stop a freight
train. The train crew put us in a sealed car. There
were police looking for vandals, maybe hoboes who
had burned a water tank at Lytton, and the crew
didn't want them to find us. We got a job with a lumber outfit near Fernie. In the spring I went to Brooks,
Alberta, got a job with two American farmers from
Carolina. Each of them owned one section and rented
another. Had a thousand head of stock—horses and
cattle. Another farmer tried to coax me away from
them with promises of better money, but I stuck with
the Americans. They used me okay. I think that was
the year we threshed in December.

For a couple of years I worked in the lumber

woods in winter, drove logs on the streams in spring, then went on harvest in the summer. When I worked in the woods I was a member of the Wobblies— Industrial Workers of the World. Best union for the men that I ever ran into. That red card meant something. I was going to buy a farm in Alberta. The farmers I worked for offered me livestock on shares. I made a down payment and went home to Nova Scotia to see my people.

I intended to go back in the spring on a homesteaders' excursion. But I went firing on the railroad up near Campbellton, met a girl there, and we were soon married. I never went back west for my down payment!"

"**WHEN WE REACHED WINNIPEG**, Roy Maxwell and I slept in a boxcar in the outskirts of the city. That night I dreamed I had found a job. We went downtown in the morning, used the only dollar we had to buy a meal. Outside the restaurant we met a man who asked, 'Are you boys working?' 'No!' 'Then you'd better come with me!' That was Sid Neill, a councillor from Milden, Saskatchewan. He gave us a job—four dollars stooking, six dollars when threshing started. Slept and ate in bunk cars. When threshing, we took turns coming in for lunch. The farmer never came out of the field during the day. When I came in for dinner I would take out a fresh team of horses for the binder. I had to depend on other fellows for the time—I had sold my watch for five dollars at a secondhand store in Sydney to make up my fare.

We couldn't work on real windy days, the stooks would fall apart. The first combine arrived that year [1928]. It was on Sunday and we all turned out to watch it. If we wanted cold water we had to take it out of the pump at night and put it in a jug and leave it outside for the night."

"**F**ROM WINNIPEG we went to Regina. No work. Went on to Wilcox. Got on with a farmer named Drew. Good place, we stayed until October—they had their own threshing outfit. When they had finished we went on to High River. We struck a bad place, though. They had a Japanese cook and the grub was hellish. We stuck it out for three weeks, though. Averaged five dollars a day wages.

The first question they fired at you anywhere: 'Where are you fellows from?' 'Nova Scotia.' 'D'you want a job?' and you had it made.

In '23 we worked for Ray Ferguson near Wilcox. It was a wet fall. For days on end we stayed in the bunk-house, just getting our board. Good food and we got into town sometimes. I could have stayed in the West, working for a farmer from Iowa on his pig farm in Saskatchewan. But I went down to the States, worked for Brown and Sharpe in Providence, Rhode Island. The plant there was full of Nova Scotians."

"**M**Y FATHER WAS A RAILROAD MAN. He got me a return pass from New Glasgow to Winnipeg, so I didn't go on the excursion train—took the regular passenger train. I was only seventeen. There was lots of work in southern Manitoba, so I went there. I got on with a French-speaking farmer—no English at all—at Notre Dame de Lourdes. I slept in the barn with the two horses. I'd never harnessed a horse, and the first morning I tried to put the collar on over a horse's head and he took off. The boss had a French-English dictionary and we tried to use it to communicate. The food was great, and some of the workers could speak

English at the table. When threshing I slept in everything from a hen house—the hens were shooed out
first—to a feather bed. At one place I slept up in the
loft on the second floor of a shack this couple had put
up in a hurry after they were burned out. One day I
helped kill a pig and ate a lot of fresh pork. I got terrible sick during the night. Now I didn't realize that after I went to my bunk the farmer and his wife put
their bed right under the trap door up to the loft, and
took the ladder down. There wasn't much room in the
shack, after all. Anyway I got fumbling around trying
the find the ladder in the dark, tumbled down on top
of them in the bed, and barfed all over them. I got fired
next day.

Did I save any money? Let me see—I had borrowed twenty-five dollars from my schoolteacher aunt
to go west, I came home with twenty-five dollars and a
new overcoat. I had no desire to stay out in that
country."

"**D**IPHTHERIA HIT ME at the first place I
worked—near Zelma—in '23. The farmer took me to a
doctor in town and he fixed me up with some shots. In
'25 a whole bunch of Scandinavians, a couple hundred
of them, hit Winnipeg before us and took a lot of jobs, I
remember they carried straw suitcases. We went on to
Biggar with what money we had, stayed in a rooming
house with some other Pictou County men. By and by
an American farmer named Crowe came looking for
men. He had hired the Scandinavians but found they
either couldn't work or didn't want to. He let them go
and hired us. Hired a Frenchman too, who was a good
worker but hated eggs.

I had a balky horse in my team, which made the
hauling rough sometimes. I recall we ate an awful lot

of chicken. It was hilly country and we had to use breeching and martingales on the teams. I think some of the horses were even shod, which horses hardly ever were out there.

It was wet for days on end. I got some sort of rheumatism in my shoulder and could scarcely work. I got some Egyptian liniment for it in town. The stuff helped my rheumatism but it ate holes in my work pants and in the bedclothes. And the alkali water was eating at my insides.

My wife came from the Magdalen Islands. Some men from there stayed with us once or twice en route to the harvest. One had his belt buckle shot off on a station platform in Quebec. They kept on to Boston and New York after the harvest, had no more desire to stay on the prairie than I did myself."

"**T**HINGS WERE BAD HERE IN '28—one or two days work in the Thorburn mine at two sixty or so a day. I knew a Prince Edward Island man running a farm in Saskatchewan and wrote to him. He gave me a job at Strasbourg, twenty miles southeast of Regina. I lived in the farmhouse, had the very best of food. Bad water until you got used to it. I stayed on the ranch until December, after getting my return ticket extended. Saved a good bit of money even though I went to town every weekend. I would like to have stayed in the West, but good land was scarce and hard to get by then."

"**I**N '24 THERE WAS A STEAM TRACTOR on the separator. Bull Fulton, a fireman on the Intercolonial Railroad at home in the old days, was fireman on it. In '25 I went west with an old hand and we got a job fast. The next year I went alone. I was wearing an Oddfellows pin. The train conductor was an Oddfellow and told me who to see in Lancer to get a job. I was too early for grain there, had to work at hay. They paid me stooking wages anyway. Terrible water out there, but fine food. George Oliver from New Annan ran a dairy farm out there. He coaxed me to stay, but I had heard too much about the terrible winters. I saved money—two years—but the crop was bad in '25.

I came back home, became a mine captain in the Malagash salt mine [now Pugwash]."

"**I RODE A TRAIN** from Winnipeg to Calgary, stayed in a hotel near the CPR station for one dollar a night. I located the employment bureau. They told me to go to Vulcan—men were needed there. Another fellow and I had enough money to help a third man to go to Vulcan too—he was broke. We worked there for Beatons. They had gone from Ontario to Wyoming, ranched there until the grass got short. Then the brothers, Dan and Neil, went north to the High River country where the grass grew higher than the neck yokes on the team.

They had a section of well-watered land. We painted the separator before threshing began. An engineer from Wichita, Kansas—he also ran a garage when home—kept the kerosene-burning Case tractor running. She started with a bar on the flywheel. Dan and Neil had two Massey-Harris binders, two McCormicks. I was used to McCormick binders and kept them in shape. They paid me one dollar a day extra for that. The fellow stooking with me, a Westerner, was too sore to work the second day. He had a lot of muscles, all aching. I had none to ache. The boss took my advance out of his wages, and he was not happy. The engineer found work for me at other places. One farmer was an

Englishman—Tom Guy. He had one hundred twenty-five cows and the same number of horses. His nineteen-year-old daughter was the cook. Then I worked for a Dutchman near Gleichen on Indian Reserve land. Millions of flies in his bachelor household. Worked at oats on Sunday there—he was no churchman. I stayed after harvest to get my money—the boss had to ship some wheat to get my wages.

In '21 my wife went out with me. Wanted to go back to Beaton's, but their crop had failed. We were hired on a ranch thirteen miles northeast of Calgary. My wife cooked for the crew. The place was owned by a Calgary businessman, who paid by the month. I saved two hundred dollars the second year, four hundred the first.

Men from New Brunswick, Nova Scotia, and British Columbia were the most in demand as harvest workers. There was one B. C. man at Beaton's. I would like to have stayed in the West—my old throat trouble cleared up completely out there."

"**I** LEFT O'LEARY, Prince Edward Island, on the narrow gauge railroad, crossed the pond, then took the excursion train in Moncton. Quiet, yes, a happy time on the train. Fight? Lord, what was there to fight about? Now there was some noise in the evening, going along the big lakes. Some of the boys had pistols, and they'd be trying them out the windows over the lake. Thought it was the thing to do to take a gun to the wild and woolly West, I guess. And we did pick a lot of blueberries and stole a little milk to go on them. No harm done.

Farm? No, not me. If I'd wanted to farm I would have stayed on the Island. No, I got a job on the CPR, worked over thirty years for them. Quite a few Island people stayed in the West. Women were teachers, men homesteaded or got on the railroad or into construction. I was on a train through the mountains east of Revelstoke one day. Except for one guy on the pusher engine, the whole train crew was from P. E. I. Yes sir, the old Island was well represented in the Pass that day. **"**

"I WORKED WITH A LARSEN, an American, a job farmer—would do any work that farmers wanted. He lived in the States but came off across the border to do custom work. He was quite independent when he came on a threshing job—brought a tankwagon of water and a load of food with him for the crew. He threshed at so much a bushel, then moved on. Seventeen teams followed—all this made a caravan about a mile long. Raised quite a dust! And that prairie dust got into your hair, your underwear, your skin, your suitcases, everywhere, as long as you were out there. I got lost one time with a team of horses, but let them find their own way to the barn. Another time I put them in the corral after work, somebody had left a gate open and they escaped. I got another harvester to drive me out next morning, found them a few miles away. I caught the tamer horse of the two, rode him back to the barn. The other one followed.

At the end of the season I bought my return ticket, was all ready to leave for home. A man came into the station saying, 'Anybody here want a job?' He said he'd give me seven fifty a day. So I cancelled my ticket and went with him. Drove his team a few days. But I got sick, got a sort of flu.

And when I was waiting to catch the train, I had to spend the night in this village. I was talking to an older man—when I say old, he was probably only thirty-five or so—I was eighteen, he seemed pretty old to me. And he said, 'Where are you going to stay?' I said, 'Apparently a hotel up here.' 'Oh,' he said, 'I wouldn't stay in the hotel, you'll get lice. You might get lousy or something—bedbugs.' Well, I didn't know anything about this sort of thing, so I didn't. I said, 'Where are you going to stay?' He said, 'I'm gonna sleep in the straw stack.' That appealed to me, so I worked into this straw stack. He told me how to do it: just burrow into the stack, then you're supposed to cover the hole. At this time of year, in October, it's getting rather cold, you know. And you cover your head like that and you stay there.

Well, I shivered all night. And the colder I got the farther in the straw stack I would go. And the farther in you go the wetter it gets. I had a terrible night, I remember still.

Anyway, the next day I was sick. So I'd been paid off and I had over two hundred dollars in my pocket. And I got aboard this colonist car again coming back to Quebec City. And I just laid on the seat most of the time. You'd get off now and again and get a light lunch at one of these stopovers, you know.

Felt a little better when the train reached Winnipeg. I got off the train, went in a shoe store to get a pair of shoes. When I took my boot off to try the shoes on there was still a lot of wheat in my boot and it spilled over the nice red carpet in the store!

I stopped to see a friend in Quebec on the way back—he was very depressed. His wife and most members of his large family had died of the flu during the two months since I had seen him before. This was in 1918. As I reached Nova Scotia I could see one house after another with quarantine signs. Guess that's what I had had in the West. I was only eighteen years old, and I had recovered.

We were always paid in cash in the West. I arrived back with two hundred dollars—ten twenty-dollar bills in my hip pocket. It was there from the time I left Saskatchewan till I got home. I put it on the table at home before my mother and father. They were quite glad to get the hard cash like that. It was quite short in supply at that time!

When I was in the West I had two attacks of severe diarrhea from alkali water—once when stooking, once when threshing.

I met no other Nova Scotians on the crews I was with.

I had no desire to stay in the West. I was a Nova Scotian, always was and always will be.

Anyway, after I arrived back home I worked in the lumber mills and lumber yards for three years. Then I saved up some money and I went to Dalhousie and studied medicine and graduated in 1927. I eventually settled in Liverpool in 1929, and stayed here until this time.

But I was on the Government Commission in the planning of Medicare. I think that was 1966 perhaps—thereabouts. We traveled across Canada. We went to Ottawa, and Toronto, and to Regina. And in Regina we traveled from Regina north over the very same fields—from Regina to Saskatoon—we traveled over the same area where I worked when I was a boy. I was then in my sixties, and when I was eighteen years old I had worked the same area riding a team of horses, threshing grain and so on. And on this commission we drove over the same area, and I recognized the country from my memory, my memories of it."

"**I WAS WITH FOUR OTHER MEN**. We went on to Weyburn. The experienced harvesters gave us lots of advice on where to go. They told us not to work, on any account, for a man from Ontario. 'He'll feed you on skim milk and the Bible,' they told us. But I worked for three outfits. Two were Americans, one was run by two brothers from Ontario. In my opinion they were the best of the bunch.

They gave us good food and didn't bother us with the Bible. At Weyburn we did what was usually done—went and sat around the grain elevators where the farmers would come in and gather. There were a lot of hoboes—many of them were IWW men [Wobblies]. They weren't still active, but they were around. If a farmer offered them work they would pretend to be insulted.

We weren't at the elevators long before somebody came and hired us. We slept in a bunkhouse. I had my own blankets from the woods. Heat and mosquitoes a nuisance, especially when we were stooking. Alkali water made us sick too. I had stooked a little oats in the East, but it was a different story out there. For the first while I couldn't keep up at all! In one place there wasn't much wheat—it was mostly wild oats, and the wind would blow the stooks over just about as fast as you'd stand 'em up.

But finally I got with the Ontario fellows west of Weyburn. They had a good outfit. I drove a bundle wagon when we started threshing. At half past four they pounded on the side of the caboose and told you to go out and feed the horses. All I took off at night was my shoes and a mackinaw jacket, so it didn't take long to dress.

I'd get out, feed and harness the horses. You were supposed to be hauled up by the separator with a load on by seven o'clock. They blew the whistle then. Three lunches they brought out to us—in the middle of the morning, at noon, and in the middle of the afternoon. You worked as long as you could see, then hit back for the barn, put the horses in, gave them a feed, then went in to supper.

The first couple of weeks I fell into my bunk right after supper. But about the third week I was getting a little friskier. Some of the boys had been in to Weyburn and bought some Niagara wine. You could buy a gallon then for a dollar and a quarter. I suppose this had been the go-ahead every weekend, but I had been too tired to realize it. I appeared in this little outbuilding and they were sitting around in a circle drinking this stuff. Now they called you, not by name, but where you came from out there. When I showed up they shouted, 'Here comes Nova Scotia! Finish it, Nova Scotia!' So I picked up this gallon jug around the crook of my arm as you do with that sort of jug, put it up and downed it. 'Glug, glug, glug!' I handed it back empty and they said, 'Jesus Christ! He did finish it!'

There were spike-pitchers in the field—sort of rovers—who would help you pitch on a load if you had any trouble. And there'd be a spike pitcher at the mill to help fork off the load faster. It took about five minutes to get your load off and into the thresher faster. With five teams on the go, one each side, you had about twenty minutes to get your load on and get back again. Used to get pretty tired. There's tricks in everything, of course. This separator we had was fairly old, and if you threw a bundle or two on sideways and then piled 'em on fast you could stog the thing. Then you'd get a little rest while they cleaned the mess out.

You daren't do it too often, of course. One day the mill was plugged, I was waiting my turn to pull in beside it and went sound asleep sitting on the front of the load. First thing I knew one of the mill men was pulling my feet and hollering, 'Wake up, Nova Scotia!'

The horses we had were broken but skittish—no shoes on them, they were barefooted, of course, and liable to bolt, especially when the whistle blew. My team did that one day, but I got them stopped by turning them into a patch of summer fallow.

Another day a fierce hailstorm hit all of a sudden—great big hailstones—when I was pulled up at the mill. My team began bucking and kicking, hurt by the egg-size stones. Three other teams all bolted, but my team was jammed up against a little granary. One horse reared up over the pole, the hamestraps broke and harness got wrapped around his front legs. I got them unhitched and freed the harness with those great big feet flying around my ears! Busiest time I ever had.

Now I didn't save much money—I had to leave early to go back to college. Suppose I got back to Fredericton with sixty dollars more than when I left.

I had an uncle had gone west some years before and became a CPR conductor. There were other Maritimers who stayed out there too—a good many went on to Alberta and British Columbia. Some men on the car I went out on were making their eighth and tenth trips to the harvest."

"**WE WERE TOLD IN WINNIPEG** that a farmer looking to hire men would have a bunch of wheat straws sticking out of his vest pocket. A Scotch farmer, Patterson, with that 'badge,' hired us. He had six hundred acres in wheat, one binder and team. He could only make one round before dinner. I slept in the house, the other men in a straw stack. I was well used there.

I didn't save any money during two months on the harvest. After it was over we wrote a Cape Bretoner then in Montana. He told us there were no jobs there. I got off at Montreal, went to the Maine lumber woods, and worked there for five years."

"MY UNCLE HAD GONE WEST in 1905 on the harvest, stayed out working as a blacksmith on the Canadian Northern Railroad. In 1926 five of us worked on the same farm near Moose Jaw. I stayed disking and hauling wheat until November. We went back there in '27, then to Bill Gardiner's place at Nobleford, Alberta. We intended to get off at another town but the Mounties turned us away—harvesters had just looted the town.

I got sixty dollars a month for disking and hauling wheat after harvest. In November I traded return tickets with a British Columbia man and started for the coast. Our train was held in Calgary all night because of a snowstorm in the mountains. When I got to Vancouver there was no work. I couldn't get into the States—had no papers to get across the border. Went back to Cape Breton."

"TWO CAMPBELLS and another MacFarlane went with me in 1921. The first farm we were on, near Vulcan, the cook was an Englishman. He couldn't cook for a bear. We beefed so bad that the boss fired him and found a good cook. Six dollars a day we got. At one farm though we couldn't get it until we got a lawyer in Calgary to collect it for us. Thirty-three dollars each we got the next spring, after the lawyer took his share.

Terrible hot and dry on the prairie—so dry I couldn't sweat."

"ANOTHER ENGLISHMAN AND I, living in Pictou County then, went out in 1910. Worked down near the American line, out of Regina. Quite a satisfactory place, though we disliked the water and there was nothing else to drink.

Coming back from town one Saturday I got lost, slept in a haystack that night. It was cold when I awakened. I made a little fire in a sheltered place away from the haystack to warm myself before trying to find my way home. By and by, what came riding across the prairie but a North West Mounted policeman. The blighter saw the smoke and came to determine whether somebody was threshing on Sunday without a permit.

I saved a bit of money. After the harvest was completed my pal went off to look for gold at Revelstoke, while I went east to work in the maple sugar camps in the Eastern Townships of Quebec. Eventually I went back to live in Jersey, in the Channel Islands."

"**S**CEPTRE, SASKATCHEWAN, out of Swift Current, was my place. I was used okay. There was a trench twelve feet wide, eight or so feet deep, running right through town. One weekend I followed it about twenty miles heading north. It ended in a place strewn with huge granite boulders, big as houses some of 'em. Old-timers told me it was an old buffalo trail and the buffalo used to use the boulders to scratch themselves.

I worked near Fillmore south of Regina in '28. One day I saw one of the last steam outfits, bunkhouse, cookhouse, twelve wagons, all painted red, crossing the prairie.

Maybe some saved money. I think most of the 'big wages' went in sprees in Winnipeg, Regina, Moose Jaw, or Montreal. Lots of young fellows learned the bad and good side of life on the harvest excursion."

"I CAME BACK!

I went out to Regina. I went on an old harvest excursion, you know. It was kind of a failure. I think I had eighty dollars when I came back. So it wasn't much better than it would have been here.

I learned one thing when I was out. If we worked as hard here as they were working out there, we'd be better off. Because I worked from five o'clock in the morning till ten at night. So I was figuring if we'd do that here, maybe we'd be better off than we were.

I wouldn't be tired or anything. I didn't like the country. The water was terrible. And it was dry. I never saw a drop of rain the whole summer I was there. And the ground drifted like snow does here in the wintertime, when it would blow. There was no sod or anything, you know.

This is the best place to live, I thought. You're only going to make a living, anyway. If you have something more than you need, it'll never be any good to you. Isn't that right?"

Angus J. MacNeil from Grand Narrows, Cape Breton, stooking sweet clover on the harvest at Rosendale, Manitoba, 1926. *(Courtesy Angus J. MacNeil, Iona)*

CHAPTER 7

The 1920s
End of the Harvest Trains

SOMETHING MORE POWERFUL than legal decisions or increased good nature caused the better pay and conditions for farm workers in the period after World War One. Prosperity had set in. Through the 1920s crops were generally good and prices were high. In 1923 the number of farmers paying income tax in the Prairie provinces was 11,656. In Saskatchewan alone 6,650 farmers paid the hated levy. In the other six provinces, including Ontario with 6,138, only 7,217 farmers paid tax on their earnings.[1]

Farmers in the West and Ontario and to a lesser extent elsewhere became involved in co-operative associations and set up their own political organizations in order to retain their new-found prosperity and increase their influence in the country's affairs. At the same time, the 1920s, industrial workers in mines, mills and lumber camps were joining radical Socialist and militant labour organizations.

The Industrial Workers of the World—IWW or "Wobblies"—came to Western Canada from the United States early in the century. Disdaining and distrusting political action, the IWW, Marxist in doctrine, welcomed all workers into a revolutionary organization that would eventually bring the capitalists to their knees by the weapon of a general strike. And, while training men for the revolution, the IWW was an extremely active and useful tool for winning immediate tangible benefits for members. Better wages and working conditions, medical services, libraries, reading rooms and rest rooms—exploited labourers came to enjoy many such improvements by joining the Wobblies.[2]

Harding Carter of Stellarton met no Wobblies while on the harvest but joined their union in the British Columbia woods. He had high praise for the way in which the IWW looked after its members. However, an Annapolis Valley man, How Dickie, encountered a Wobbly spike-pitcher who tried to get How to start a slowdown movement: "Take it easy! Slow down!" he said. "Go to Hell!" was How's reply. Somebody apparently squealed to the farmer and the slowdown artist soon disappeared.

Another militant left-wing organization, the One Big Union [OBU] was active in the 1920s. They fomented a strike among harvesters in Manitoba in 1921. Grain was left rotting in the fields when farmers refused to meet workers' demands. In desperation the farmers had scabs brought in from the United States, swearing them to refuse any union affiliation.[3]

The IWW was blamed for burning grain fields and sabotaging machinery in Alberta. At one time Mounted Police checked the activities of IWW organizers on a threshing crew near Yorkton.[4] A piece of feeble fiction in *The Grain Growers Guide* credited Mounted Police Secret Service agents with foiling an IWW attempt at sabotaging a thresher.[5]

It has been suggested that the stepping-up of police patrols on excursion trains after 1920 was motivated by the government's desire to "protect" excursionists from "Red agitators" at station stops. While the Mounties were not averse to labour-bashing or left-wing witch hunts, this theory seems a bit far-fetched. No harvester ever mentioned the presence of "agitators" of any kind at the Ontario stops. They would likely have been trampled by a horde of men desperate for food and drink.

Some of the harvesters themselves were active union men and Socialists at home, and made their influence felt in the West. Tom McEwen (or Ewen), a Communist district organizer in Winnipeg, learned his first lessons in socialist philosophy and working-class action from harvesters.[6]

ALL VERY WELL. But the Maritime harvesters interviewed were all zealous supporters of the work ethic. There was a competitive spirit in the harvest workers, especially on threshing crews. Men would work like fiends to keep up with the crew. And, as Maurice MacDonald said, "It was to our advantage to get the crop harvested; hell, our families had to eat, after all!" And the Maritimers were convinced that their work was highly valued. Farmers apparently were shrewd group psychologists like football coaches: they told the Maritimers that they were the best workers that ever hit the Prairies. And the Easterners were convinced that it was true. George Haythorne maintained, though, that the British Columbia men were the most sought after by farmers. They "were mainly men who had previous agricultural experience. Since they were also Westerners, used to Western ways, they were usually at a premium on the prairie grain fields."[7]

IF, HOWEVER, there had been prizes for the most ineffective and inept of all groups of harvesters, there is no doubt they would go to the British harvesters who came out on three occasions in the 1920s. Herb Dickeson again:

"A big crowd of Englishmen were taken over one year, promised big wages. Mostly they couldn't get jobs; if they did get work they got the lowest wages. They couldn't even harness a horse—they expected 'barnmen' to put the harness on and take it off! They were no good at all—a lot of them had to be helped by government to go back to England."

A Canadian trade union official who had been twice on the excursion himself described the incursion of Britishers in 1928 as a triumph of deceit—"the greatest crime ever inflicted on a body of men." The men had been deceived and hoodwinked by promises of a whole summer of work at good pay.[8]

There seems to be no doubt that the nearly 8500 overseas miners who came to the harvest in 1928 were completely unprepared for the work. Years of unemployment, poor food, and class hostility had left them physically weak and festering with hatred for all employers. Desperation drove them to apply for the harvest emigration when recruiting efforts in Eastern Canada met initially with little response. Coming across the ocean, they were apparently bombarded with speeches and literature by Communist agitators assuring them the whole scheme was a swindle "to get rid of many British workers so capitalism could grind the rest more easily."[9]

An earlier mass incursion by British workers in 1923 was reasonably successful—only 21 per cent of the almost 12,000 who came over went back to Britain at the end of the season.[10] Many of the 1923 migrants had agricultural experience, however.

It's only fair to note that the poor Britishers encountered a huge body of prejudice that had built up in the prairie West against English "greenhorns." Such "Limeys" were a favourite target of Bob Edwards' broad humour: remittance men paid to leave their country for the country's good and sending home outrageous lying tales of the West; ignorant and awkward English tenderfeet impervious to advice; the West saw more than its share of such before 1914. Many of them left their bones in France during the Great War. They may have been a bit green, said Bob Edwards, but they were never yellow.[11]

George Haythorne goes against most other commentators when he calls the majority of the 1928 crowd of Britishers "efficient workers...a valuable increment to the labour force."[12] But there can be no argument that as an experiment in assisted immigration the 1928 "invasion" of British workers was a failure. Ninety per cent of them returned to the British Isles.[13]

AS FAR AS THAT GOES the assisted emigration of Maritimers as permanent settlers to the Prairies was practically a failure also. During the 1920s, seventy-nine per cent of harvesters from Eastern Canada went home after the harvest. Prairie businessmen complained that the Down Easters made their money in the West and spent it back home.[14] Probably, as already mentioned, more Maritimers remained in the West before land prices rose sharply in World War I. But overall, the interviews show that they feared the long cold winters, the isolation, the lack of winter employment. And if they went home with the idea of coming back to settle, their women would be very cool toward the idea.

Not only had they heard returning harvesters tell

of the discomforts of western life—and the stories grew with the telling—but the women read stories in *The Family Herald* and other journals—accounts of western blizzards, of wolves, of sod shacks with no conveniences and no neighbours within miles.[15] If John wanted that sort of life, Mary did not. If they had to leave, far better to head for Boston, Providence, or Detroit, where friends and relatives had already taken root. And the Scots and Irish who made up a very significant fraction of the Maritime population were not wedded to farm life anyway. They had put up with it in pioneering days when there was no alternative, when the ownership of fields and woods in the new land was a vast improvement over the situation in the old homelands which had been taken from them.

BUT IN FULFILLING the immediate objective of the excursions—saving the grain crop—the Maritimer did very well. In a sort of Jekyll-and-Hyde transformation, the rambunctious Easterners who left a trail of destruction from Moncton or Saint John to Winnipeg settled down and performed splendidly on prairie farms. They thought of themselves as team players in a great national enterprise.

The harvest excursions, however, came to an abrupt end in 1928. That was the second largest ever organized. No more excursions from Maritime points took place after that year, though individual excursion tickets were seasonably available until 1969. The 1928 excursion was followed in 1929 by the smallest excursion since 1900—but *those* harvesters came from Ontario and Quebec. There may have been Maritimers among them. But there were no harvest trains from the Maritimes after 1928.

"The immediate reason for reducing the number

of harvesters to fewer than 4000 in 1929 was a partial crop failure."[16]

Crop failures continued. There was little grain to harvest and no money to pay workers.

Drought, Debt, and Depression plagued the Prairies. Within a few years the rails which had borne trainloads of harvesters carried another kind of cargo into the Prairies—food and clothing—relief supplies from the eastern provinces for needy families on western farms.

Harvesting operations underway, circa 1910.
(Courtesy Provincial Archives of Manitoba)

APPENDIX A

Steve Whitty
A Story and a Song

"Going to the Harvest"

Come all you boys of In-go-nish and lis-ten to my song. You know I am no po-et so I can-not make it long. I'm act-ing on a trip we had to the wild west we did steer, In search of our for-tune which you will quick-ly hear.

MIKE MACDOUGALL'S FATHER—Dan Rory—he was the awfullest man ever to make up a song about you. He made one there about where we went to the harvest in 1920. People had been going for years and years before that. That was the first year I went. I was twenty-three. In my prime of life.

At that time you'd sail over to North Sydney on the first *Aspy* and buy your train ticket—twenty-eight dollars and a quarter from North Sydney to Winnipeg—one way. Before we left Ingonish, you'd be hearing the talk of it. Oh, they'd be there and meeting you, to get you to go to work for them. Dan Rory's song went:

"It being on the fourth of August we left our friends so dear/ On board the steamboat *Aspy* for Sydney we did steer/ It being on the evening of the fifth our tickets we produced/ To take us all to Winnipeg, that place that we all cursed."

Because when we got there we couldn't get a job. And we were shy on money. You had to get grub enough in North Sydney, and you know what that was like after a few days in an old suitcase. It was that hard it was like bullets. My dear soul.

There were jobs in Winnipeg. But we went too early. It wasn't our fault. That was the time that was advertised in the papers. There was no place for food along the way, really, you couldn't get anything. You'd get the train stopping here and there, and a little store—get a bottle of pop or something like that. We were dying for that. The water was awful on the train.

"We travelled for six days and nights, our provision it got slim/ And to get off the iron horse we sure were in bad trim/ Both sleepy, dirty, and hungry, we scarcely could crawl/ And to be without cold water, we found the worst of all."

There were 820 on our train. And there was 800 on a train three-quarters of an hour after. But when we got to Winnipeg there was nothing to do. All seven of us could have got on, but they only offered us the smallest kind of wages. Because harvesting hadn't started and they thought they had us right there.

Some fellows on the street told us the harvest had got started in Moose Jaw, Saskatchewan. That was four hundred miles from Winnipeg. But still and all, you could go that four hundred miles for two dollars—half a cent a mile was the rate. We went to Moose Jaw.

"Oh Jim, he was quite nervous, as any you ever saw/ He bid goodbye to Tom and Frank when we landed in Moose Jaw/ 'May the Lord above look down,' he said, 'have mercy unto me/ For here we are both one and all, no work that I can see.'"

When we got there it was the same damn thing. Harvesting hadn't started. So there we were, the seven of us on the street. "Now Jack he was quite surly, and unto us did say/ 'Oh pity my condition and warning take by me/ If my father had done justice when first out west I roamed/ And taken down the shotgun and broke some of my bones.'"

By and by we saw a fellow coming toward us. Asked us were

we looking for work. Told him yes. "We walked along on Main Street all looking for a job/ We met a man who said to us, 'Go get on the waterworks/ I'll pay you five dollars a day, charge forty cents for meals/ You will not go a-harvesting if you'll accept this deal.'"

That didn't leave us a hell of a lot, but we were satisfied to go. But it was a bad place to work. "We went to work next morning in that Godforsaken place/ Nothing but French Canadians, and the flies, they'd eat your face/ Down in the hole went Frank and Jack, in mud and mar they strayed/ Which caused them to look around, say, 'A damn short time we'll stay.'"

Every evening we'd go out to see if we could find out anything about the harvesting. "It was in that place of poverty we lasted for five days/ There was no place else to eat or sleep, not even to wash your face/ It was then we took the notion, another job to hunt/ We went to seek and we did meet the man they call Beaumont."

The boss we hired with in the harvest said he would give us six dollars a day and free board and free bed. We had a great place there. Didn't work hard at all. The work was stooking the grain. It was all cut by machinery. It would go on this rake and it all went in sheaves and it was tied and thrown out. And you came along and stooked them together. Leave them standing in the field to ripen. We only had two jobs, stooking and threshing. After the grain was all ripened on the stalks, we had two horses each to haul it in to where they were threshing it. Wonderful experience. I never forgot it nor I ever will, because I loved it.

But I went to the harvest just the once. For us, that was the end of the harvest train. It was awful going out there. I enjoyed it because there was a bunch of us good fellows together. But there was some of them awful, for stealing and breaking in stores and things like that. The people were frightened to death. I don't see why they didn't shoot them. They fired out everything. All sorts of clothes. Boxes of shoes and everything else. And you know those small buckets of jam—well, boy, anybody on the train wanted jam could get it with no trouble. Carry loads of that aboard the train.

Train would start in North Sydney. There were twenty-two cars. And it was breaking in and stealing from the time we left. Because some that were on the train were used to this, were at it before. They would tell the conductors where they wanted to stop, and the poor fellows would have to stop. God knows what they wouldn't do. I'm not telling you a lie. I've seen them going out and bringing aboard the train God knows how many hens they took out of a hen house. And when the train was going as fast as ever she could go—fastest I ever saw was forty-eight miles an hour—because the mileage was on posts and that's all you had to do, everyone had a watch, seeing how many miles we were going an hour. Anyway, bring those poor hens in and they wouldn't kill them—they'd let them go. Fire them out through the windows. One by one you'd see the hens go. The poor things. These were mostly young fellows.

Not saying everyone did this. No, no, no. Just two, say, in the car I was in. And they would get together wherever the train would stop. But after we crossed Quebec Bridge, the soldiers were there lined up with their guns. "Now you touch one of these stores and we'll touch you." There was no more stealing after we crossed Quebec Bridge. They had soldiers right along, wherever they slowed down for coal and water and things like that—the soldiers would be there. And it's a good thing the stealing stopped because the cars were already piled up with things they never used. Neckties, shirts, shoes—boxes of little kids' shoes— shoes with copper toes. See they were no good, fire them away.

(*What did you do that was bad?*) Well, I suppose I did my share. But I didn't do any stealing, I can tell you that. I never took anything. I had a dread over me. I was twenty-three and there were lots there only seventeen and they didn't know what badness meant. You could talk to people and tell them it wasn't right to be bringing hens and stuff like that in the train—which we did. They'd just laugh at you.

(*If this was the case, I'm surprised the harvest trains kept running.*) Stopped after that year. She never took anyone, only students going to college after that. They weren't allowing any-one to go who was on the train before. Then they started getting better gear on the fields and now I don't think even the college boys are going.

(*And you say it was a wonderful experience. How could it be so good? You went out too early, food was all ruined, had to work on the waterworks, and then you were just lucky to get some harvest work....*) Yeah, it was all luck. (*And that was the best job you ever had?*) Well, it was the best job I ever had with a boss onto it. He was just like a father to us all. Told us he'd give us six dollars a day and free board—and when he paid us off, he paid us off with seven. Straight time. So he was a good guy. Seven dollars a day in 1920 was big money.

I went there in August—I think the twelfth of August we hired on—and my brother-in-law, Mike's father—he and I came home the last of October. A little over two months. And I had something clear over four hundred dollars. Went with nothing but my fare. And Dan Rory put at the end of the song:

"So now my song is over, no more I have to say/ But we will soon be going back to that place we call South Bay/ Our boats and trawls we'll outfit, for the eastern piece prepare/ To get us some provision and some clothing for to wear."

Dan Rory would come in here now, sit around sizing up you and I. That's what he'd done, "Going to the Harvest." Had twenty-two verses in that song, "Going to the Harvest." And I never knew he was doing it. When we were still there, he just worded it for me. He didn't have it finished. "There's none left but Dan and Steve, the harvest for to win/ We would not disappoint the man or leave him in bad trim."

Oh, songs were our entertainment. Indeed they were. And there was a great deal of singing in that home. Oh, my dear man. And you know, people don't do this anymore. There's not the gimp enough in them anymore. What I call gimp, well, you've got to be full of life.

APPENDIX B

Jane MacKay Rutherford
from *I Came from Pictou County: Recollections of a Prairie Bluenose*

WHEN I FIRST STARTED TEACHING, at sixteen, for $90 a year, the Reverend Mrs. J. W. Fraser had taken me aside and advised, "Be sure and put some money in the bank." Money in the bank! If you had a spare quarter, you put it in the bank. At the end of those four years of teaching, I had plenty of money in the bank! And at the end of those four years, I went west!

WHY DID I GO WEST? Well, I was young—everyone was doing it—there was more money. Teachers were paid $700 a year in the west and that was more than $270. But there was something besides that. When I was very small I remember Father reading letters from the *Colonial Standard*—that was the Pictou paper, a Tory paper, before the *Advocate*. He often used to read aloud to us. And he always used to read the letters in the *Standard* from the Reverend George Roddick who had gone out from Durham, Pictou County, to Brandon, Manitoba. In all those letters there was a recurrent phrase, "the blue hills of Brandon." It appealed to me, somehow, "the blue hills of Brandon." Later, when I was at the Academy, Mr. Roddick himself came home from Brandon and married his childhood sweetheart, a Miss Logan. We used to see him, a little trim man with a cane, coming down the street. In my Regina days, and later here in Saskatoon, the name "Roddick" seemed to follow me. As for the letter writer, Mr. Roddick himself, I heard that when he died they took his body back west to lie beside that of his first wife—back to the hills of Brandon.

It wasn't until 1914 when I went east to Nova Scotia with Dad, that I looked for the "blue hills of Brandon." In a way, I think it was the Reverend George Roddick's blue hills that drew me to the west long before I had any notion of going.

No, I didn't go west to be a pioneer. I had no idea that what I was doing would ever be considered "pioneering." A pioneer? Goodness, no! I don't think we ever used such a word about ourselves in those days. And no, your father never thought of himself as a pioneer, either. And he certainly didn't think of himself as going out to experience hard times when he went out west from Ontario in 1906. *No!* It was an opportunity. It was a great adventure.

The old people, our forefathers, now—*those* were the pioneers. I remember the old orchard in Nova Scotia—was it west, north of us? I don't remember. There were no directions in Nova Scotia; nothing was ever straight as on the prairie. In this orchard was an old gnarled apple tree, the hardest looking pill of a tree—stick-coloured, only a quarter of it left. Still, it bore apples. It must have been over a hundred years old. Mar'n Munroe used to tell us—Mar'n was near eighty then—she lived in the little shingled house across the road where Mrs. Graham lived with all the cats in later years, though the house had been Hughie Campbell's first—Mar'n used to tell us that her father and mother slept by that tree under sheets of bark, hemlock bark, when they first came out from Scotland. Later they built their house nearby, and when we were young only the cellar of that house remained.

A tree had sprung up by it and we called that tree the "Cellar" tree. I suppose you could say that both the hard looking tree and the Cellar Tree marked the first shelter and dwelling of the real pioneers.

But I don't think that our forefathers, either, thought of themselves as having such hard times in this country. It wasn't all that much harder than they—the MacKays, the MacKenzies, Sutherlands, Campbells—had been used to. Yes, it must have been hard to see their roofs cut down and their houses tumbled in the Highland clearances, but the same thing is being done here today in Saskatoon in the name of progress. This year forty-nine properties were expropriated and removed to make way to the Idylwyld bridge and the householders were given only a token compensation. Not enough for those who are old to buy other houses. They're still clearing people out of the cities today, just as the landlords did in the days when our forefathers came to Pictou County.

"...THE COUNTRY WAS GREEN and everyone was young."

We left on the harvest excursion train from Scotsburn station on August 10th, 1910, fifty-five years ago today. There was a big crowd gathered to see us off. Ten or eleven of us were going— teachers, not harvesters. Olive and Edna Reid from Plainfield were both there; they were going out to Saskatchewan to teach, and to join their sister Florence who was already teaching in the west. And Jessie Munsie who had been born at the foot of Greenhill with us too. We had all joined the excursion—no, we hadn't read about it in the *Colonial Standard* or any of the papers, there were no advertisements for it that year that I remember. It was just that everyone was doing it. It was the thing to do—go west.

No, I can't remember what I was wearing on August 10th, 1910—nothing unusual, I suppose. I had a big new trunk and had lots of dresses in it. Dresses were cheap then, and I'd been teaching four years and had money in the bank. My sister Phemie had made some dresses for me; there was a black velvet for good, I know. And I had several skirts; with them I wore shirtwaists, buttoned up the back, high necked, lace or stitching down the front. We bought them in Baillie's in Pictou for seventy-five cents. Now that you ask, I remember I did wear side-buttoned boots and had button hooks in my luggage. I didn't see the high-laced boots like those your first prairie teacher wore, until much later, in the '20s. And black stockings—yes, we always wore black stockings then, though once I did have a pair of lacy brown ones—white ones were for weddings. And my hair—well, it was piled up under my hat. You could buy a big, wide hat from the milliner in Pictou for $1.50 then, and I always liked hats. I had lots of hair to pile up; when I braided it in two pigtails the braids were so long I could sit on them. Usually I piled my hair over rats, which were sausage shapes of human hair, and then I anchored my hat on top of that. If I had known that the day was going to be so important, that the harvest excursion was going to take me out west and leave me there, I might have remembered more about what I wore; but I didn't. One thing, though, I was adequately covered. There were no slacks, no shorts, no short skirts then, I can tell you. We were *well* covered, head to foot.

Appendix B: Jane MacKay Rutherford

I had bought my ticket—I thought it was about $10, but it must have been more, for the figures for 1911, which you looked up, were $16.75 for a single fare from Halifax to Winnipeg, $22.75 return. The ten or eleven of us from Scotsburn were all in one car; we took along blankets and pillows for there was no place to sleep but on the slatted seats. We also took a suppy of food. There were burners at the end of the car to make tea or do a little cooking.

"Harvest excursion" was a term that had a bad name en route to the west and Maritimers had a bad reputation. Carloads in other years had done desperate things, like tying a cow to the train or hauling a mower on to the tracks, and at some Ontario stops the excursioners would descend from the cars and loot the shops. I don't know that the Maritimers were always responsible, but they were certainly always blamed, and the villagers along the main line of the CPR dreaded the arrival of the harvest excursion trains. Our car was peaceable, though I remember one incident. When we were at a stop in northern Ontario where a store had been looted in previous excursions, someone knocked on our windows and warned us about the angry townspeople, "Don't get out! They've got guns and are ready to shoot." So we stayed where we were. Some of our travellers had mouth organs and one had a violin, so we sang and amused ourselves very well in our car without committing any atrocities.

Sometimes for amusement and exercise we walked through the long string of cars, not all of them excursion cars. Many were immigrant cars, and so many of them they seemed to stretch back to Halifax. I had my first glimpse of many newcomers, with their strange languages and appearance. It wasn't like Scotsburn where we were all Scottish except for the Fitzpatricks....

The weather was lovely that August of 1910—golden weather. It was like that all through the eastern provinces; I remember how beautiful the elms were in the sunlight in the Ottawa valley. It was perfect weather the whole five and one-half days, all the way through to Regina. As we entered Saskatchewan the girls, Jessie, Olive and Edna, dropped off one by one along the main line, Jessie Munsie at Moosomin, and another further west. Amy Cairns had written me to come to Langbank where they were now living and get a school there, but Langbank wasn't on the main line so I went into Regina and consulted the

Teachers' Agency there. Lajord—that's where they sent me—to Badger Hill school at Lajord.

IT WAS EVENING when the train pulled in to Lajord. A young man, a trustee, met me. Charlie Blish was his name; he was an American from Iowa, he was smoking a cigar and he drove a democrat pulled by two fiery horses. "Democrat" was an American name for what we called an "express" in Scotsburn. But I wasn't the only teacher waiting for him. The Agency had made a mistake and sent Charlie Blish two teachers. The other girl told him she was from Regina. As for me, I said that I was from Pictou County in Nova Scotia. Charlie Blish didn't hesitate. He took his cigar from his mouth and pointed it at me. "I'll take you," he said, "you've come furthest."

We drove out in the August night, sixteen miles into the prairie. Far away, finally, I saw a peek of light and in time I was setting foot in the Blish home. It was a house like a granary, one room below, no paint, no paper, no finished walls, just bare studding. A ladder led to a sort of loft.

Mrs. Blish senior (Charlie's mother) was a stern woman with an accent. I liked her daughter-in-law better, but the old lady ruled the roost. I remember supper that night—there was pie, a sort of cream pie. Flies lit on it in clusters and lifted it from the table. We drank green tea which I had never tasted before and I found it repulsive. As I ate supper I noticed the nails driven into the uprights to hang clothes, and the tiny granary-like windows which were never opened. There was a crock churn behind one of the doors; it was always very sour smelling and buzzing with flies. It was rarely washed out. A rough, rickety stair went up through a hole in the ceiling. It led to the room I was to share with Mrs. Blish senior and her grandchild. We waited to eat that night, I remember, until Matt, the hired man, came in with the stone boat. I wondered what in the world a "stone boat" was. Later, I saw Matt coming in across the field, feet planted wide apart on this little platform, reins held short, behind the horse. There were no "stone boats" in Pictou County; we always called them "drags."

It was lonesome that night; I think I cried. The rough, stern old woman, the sight of the dishes washed in a pan on the stove, the two or three men eating the fly-swarming pie and talking in

Iowa accents about life back home—all their talk was about "huskin corn and raisin hawgs," the old woman herself, so critical—"Oh Ma'am," she told me, "if ever you lived under a president, you'd never again want to live under a king"—all this was strange and unsettling.

When we went upstairs, climbing the ladder, I found a room divided by a curtain which was an old bed sheet. Two beds were in one corner. Here slept the old lady and her small granddaughter. The other bed was mine. There was a small window in each gable, both of them closed against the prairie air. It was different from Scotsburn where the curtains were always moving in the breeze. When I woke in the morning, the old woman looked at me accusingly. "I heard you last night," she said, "I heard you nestlin', all right."

There wasn't much in the room below, but there *was* a coffee grinder; I heard it working away early next morning. When the coast was clear, the women would call up to me and I would come down and wash at the basin. Baths? We never took them. Oh, we had sponge baths all right—but none to sit in. When I wanted a good wash I borrowed the basin and took it up to the loft.

The Blishes had come from Iowa where they were used to wind storms, so they had built a cyclone cave, a dug-out near the house. They hopped into this in heavy wind storms and generally used it as a storehole. North of the house was a cemetery enclosed with rough board slabs. Two or three of Charlie Blish's children were buried there. All around the yard, looking exactly like the house, were the granaries. The men slept in these.

The next day, Sunday, Charlie took me to see Badger Hill school, five miles away. He took me and the two children in the democrat pulled by the ex-broncos. On the way he enlightened me about the name of the province. "Saskatchewan," he said, was the wrong word. It should have been "Saskatchewaten." With that we stopped, for we had arrived at a construction camp and Charlie wanted to go in to see if he could supply them with meat. He simply dropped the reins on the dashboard and abandoned me and the children to the ex-broncos. I didn't know enough then to be afraid. The broncos didn't stir.

Badger Hill was a cottage-type school, painted, new. There had been a teacher there for two or three months. After that first

Sunday when Charlie drove me there to show me where the school was, I walked. That had been my first and only ride to school. When it was wet weather I used to carry home half a section of gumbo on my feet. Often the little Blish children would come to meet me in the evening and it would be six o'clock before we were home to the flies, the churn and the talk of corn and hawgs. It was lovely, though, that fall...there were many mirages; the horizons lifted and you imagined you saw towns, towns that weren't really there, across the fields....

You could see for miles—the prairie was level as a floor. You could see everything. One time Matt invited me to go walking to see one of the threshing rigs out on the field. Old Mrs. B. was very annoyed with me. "You should never go out like that," she scolded. "Imagine! Walking with a man on the prairie!" She had an evil mind. I wondered what in the world could happen to anyone who was always in full sight of everyone else walking out on the prairie....

What did I teach? Well, the same sort of things you took in school—the subjects that we had at Scotsburn in Pictou County. Singing? No, I never taught singing. No use doing something you couldn't do....

The prairie? I liked it. It reminded me of a poem in one of our old readers:

These are the gardens of the desert, these
The unshorn fields, boundless and beautiful,
For which the speech of England has no name—
The prairies, I beheld them for the first,
And my heart swells...

Yes, I liked them. Though there were lots of times you felt like running away. But you never did. You never could....

I THEN WENT TO NORMAL SCHOOL to get my teaching license. The classes were held in an old school; we did quite a lot of practice teaching, and I remember that when you crossed Garnet Street to go to one of the schools, you found yourself in open fields. When we did our practice teaching, a Normal School instructor and other students watched. Once I thought they were going to turn me right out of Normal. When we came back from teaching one day—I had been doing the teaching—the instructor asked if anyone had "noticed something about Miss MacKay"...in case they hadn't, they were to watch me next day, in practice, and see. I was terribly worried, wondering what I had done, or what habits I had that would make me unsuitable for teaching. Finally I coaxed one of the girls to tell me what this dreadful thing was that he wouldn't mention to me. "Your eyes," she said. "He told us to notice your eyes. He said you taught with your eyes." That was a relief. We had been having a lesson by playing a game, "Animal, Vegetable or Mineral." I guess I had been throwing myself into the game too and enjoying it...anyway, the instructor wanted to use me as an example of how to throw yourself into teaching. I was quite relieved that that was all there was to it.

That January there was a public meeting in Regina and the Normal School staff encouraged us all to attend. Nellie McClung was on the platform; she wore a long old-rose tea gown and read parts out of her *Sowing Seeds in Danny*. Mr. and Mrs. Motherwell were also on the platform; he was then the Minister of Agriculture in Laurier's government. Both of them spoke and that was the first time I had ever heard of the practice of budgeting—household budgeting. For that was Mrs. Motherwell's topic—the importance of the "budget"....

YOU'RE CURIOUS ABOUT how I met your father—well, it was this way: there were bachelors on the prairie in those days, lots of them. And a bachelor's life on the homestead wasn't bad at all—if he was like your father he had no dog, no cat, no hen, no cow—nothing really to tie him down at all. Many bachelors used canned milk in their tea and they often bought bread from a neighbour, though some of them made their own. Occasionally they wandered over to their neighbour's to be sociable or to borrow something. And that was how, a night or two before I started teaching at Butte View school, I met your father. He came in to borrow something, what I can't remember; it certainly wasn't bread or milk since he used canned milk and always got his bread from Mrs. Kerr. Anyway, he came into the McConnells' big room. He has told you how he came in to find the new teacher sitting on the couch with one leg tucked up underneath her. Sitting with one leg tucked under one may not have been quite proper, perhaps, but that's how it was. And that was how I met John Percy Rutherford, formerly of South Monaghan, Northumberland County, Ontario. His shack was about a mile south of the Macs in the north-east corner of the section.... Oh, the Saskatchewan survey system—how Mrs. Mac enjoyed it! It was her favourite puzzle, figuring out where people lived. She'd sit, screwing up her face, seeing the area laid out on the survey map in her imagination. She liked locating people on it. "Let's see, who's on that quarter?" she'd say, or "...now he must be on the north-west quarter, section 24, etc. etc." It was a game with her, locating people on an imaginary map—she could place them all the way to Chaplin. Anyway, Johnny, as she called him, was on the north-east corner of section 22, township 21, range 5, west of the 3rd meridian; and had been homesteading there for the past five years when I met him that night as I was sitting on my foot....

Top: Harvest crew, possibly in the Cromer district, Manitoba, circa 1900.
Bottom: Harvesting scene near Emerson, Manitoba.
(Courtesy Provincial Archives of Manitoba)

APPENDIX C

The Old Harvest Train

Vincent J. MacDonald

"**A**LL ABOARD THAT'S GOING ABOARD!**" So shouted the conductor of a fifteen-car passenger train at the railroad station in Antigonish at 2:00 P.M. on August 6, 1920. The train was a special headed for Winnipeg and carrying young men from eastern Canada to help the farmers of the prairie provinces harvest their grain crops—and this was quite a task as there were no tractors or combines in those days. The return fare from Antigonish to Winnipeg was $12, and for anyone going further west than Winnipeg, it was one cent per mile extra—hardly enough to pay for the damages done to railroad property by the potential harvesters.

In order to encourage men to travel westward to the prairie advertisements appeared in many local papers stating that cheap meals would be provided enroute but it turned out that the only thing that was cheap about the meals was the quality. Although the quality was low, the price was high thus causing much dissension among the would-be harvesters who, at times, resorted to many unorthodox means of securing food. In one town in New Brunswick, a food peddler who approached the standing train with a carriage load of edibles and who, no doubt, had visions of making a handsome profit on the sale of his products was quickly relieved of a large portion of his cargo by the hungry harvesters who told him that they would pay him when they were on their way back home as they were short of ready cash at the time.

At Riviere du Loup in Quebec the harvesters were not content with attempting to secure food in an unscrupulous manner; they also added beer to their list of requirements. But when they raided an establishment which illegally dispensed beer, they were met by a hail of bullets fired over their heads which had the effect of causing them to retreat to the safety of their railroad cars. Later, after having crossed the river at Levis and while their train was changing engines, the harvesters under the cover of darkness and without the discouraging sound of gunfire broke open the door of a boxcar which contained many barrels packed with beer bottles. They quickly rolled the barrels out of the car onto the ground and those bottles which did not break were readily transferred to the safety of the upper bunks of the harvest train. Needless to say, there was no problem in obtaining the necessary help to carry out this all important chore.

With such a large quantity of beer secretly stored away, the harvesters were ready to proceed along their way. They did not arise early the next morning but when they did, their appetites seemed to be keener than ever so that at the first train stop where there was a restaurant, the proprietor thereof was quickly introduced to the self service method of dispensing food and other necessities such as cigars, cigarettes, apples, oranges—for that matter, anything that the ambitious harvesters thought they could use. The turnover of those goods was fast but the profit on the transactions was less than nil.

This self-service method of securing food was repeated on many occasions but it was not the only method employed by the now experienced harvesters to relieve their hunger. On the barrens of northern Quebec, there were at this time many acres of land which produced an abundance of blueberries; and when some of the scouts appointed by the harvesters observed an exceptionally good area of blueberries, another appointee would arrange to stop the train by applying the emergency brakes. Then all the harvesters would take off to the blueberry fields and would not return to their train, despite the urging of many whistle blows, until their beer-incited stomachs were well satisfied.

In order to stop the many raids on the places of business, the railroad authorities arranged to have the harvest train disconnected from the engine about a mile from any point where the train was scheduled to stop. This procedure worked successfully for a short time. But the harvesters, responding to their hunger pangs, soon found a solution to this problem by loading the cars with rocks and timber that would be thrown at the windows of the station. Obviously this had only to occur a few times when normal traveling procedure was again followed.

Having solved the food problem and no doubt encouraged by the superb quality of the beer obtained at Levis, Quebec, the harvesters undertook the finding of ways and means of providing enjoyable pastimes. At one train stop this enjoyment took the form of unhitching a team of horses from a farmer's mowing machine and tying the machine behind the last car of the train. When the train started to move, sparks began to fly from the old Buckeye machine, but after traveling about one hundred yards the sparks died out—all but the spark in the farmer's eyes.

At Kapuskasing, Ontario, which was at the time of the First World War the location of a German prisoner-of-war camp, the harvesters did not have things all their own way. After having looted a restaurant and set fire to several haystacks, a number of natives appeared, well armed with rifles and shotguns. Needless to say, the unarmed harvesters scurried to the shelter of the railroad cars—but not before two men were caught in the hail of fire from the rifles and shotguns which also sprayed the rail road cars with bullets. Luckily, the two men were not severely injured. One had a bullet wound in the calf of his leg and he was dropped off at the first town in which a hospital was located. The other man had been sprayed with duck shot in a part of his anatomy which was not too vulnerable.

Some volunteers carried this man back to the caboose of the train, and after an examination it was decided that the pellets could be removed. But in order to proceed with this delicate operation, it was necessary to have a strong disinfectant and also a sedative to calm the patient. After several consultations, it was agreed that a quantity of moonshine which had been acquired in one of the numerous raids on business establishments would serve both purposes. The patient was informed that he would have to consume about eight ounces of the moonshine before the painstaking task of removing the pellets began. This he did willingly. Then after the elapse of about ten minutes more moonshine was applied to the affected area. Toothpicks dipped in iodine were the only "surgical" instruments available to the volunteers. Even so, after several minutes many pellets had been removed despite the fact that many of the toothpicks broke and despite the fact that the patient was beginning to recover from the effects of the sedative available. This having been done, the volunteers again proceeded to remove the remaining pellets. This was accomplished in about one-half hour, and it was never decided who was more exhausted—the patient or the volunteers. At any rate, after the elapse of about three days the patient was able to sit down as he should. As for the volunteers, the remainder of the moonshine soon solved the problem of their exhaustion.

In many of the towns of northern Ontario, particularly in the towns of O'Brien and Hearst, the windows of stores and restaurants were boarded up by the time the harvest train arrived; and in some places men armed with rifles stood inside those establishments in order to prevent looting.

On the last day of the journey, the harvesters thought that things should look somewhat respectful when the train arrived at Winnipeg. With this goal in mind, several volunteers secured a large number of spruce trees, each about ten feet in length. Those trees were firmly attached to the four corners of each car, which were fifteen in number, so that when the train reached Winnipeg it caused much consternation among the natives who doubtless were not aware of the decorative powers of the wild men from the east.

The trip from Antigonish to Winnipeg took six full days but probably if it were not for the beer and the blueberries, five days would have been sufficient.

Having arrived in Winnipeg, the potential harvesters dispersed. Some stayed to work in Manitoba, others proceeded to Saskatchewan and Alberta. Many were destined to never return to their "native land."

The work in the harvest fields was very difficult, especially for those men not accustomed to that type of work. But the wages paid were good. The hours of labor were long, particularly at threshing time—generally from 4:30 A.M. to 8:00 P.M., sometimes even later than that if a big snowstorm was threatening. But even though the work was hard and the hours long, as a general rule the men were treated well. The food was the very best, and during the long hours at threshing the men were fed four or five times per day.

After the harvesting and threshing was over, it was a case of every man for himself. Some returned to their homes in the east. Others proceeded to British Columbia and still others to

Appendix C: The Old Harvest Train

Butte, Montana, which at one time was a second home to the young men of Antigonish County. The writer of this article kept on the move and eventually after eight years landed back at the starting point—the Antigonish railroad station.

Steam threshing near Portage La Prairie, 1900.
(Courtesy Provincial Archives of Manitoba)

Harvesters at the CPR Station, Winnipeg, circa 1900.
(Courtesy Provincial Archives of Manitoba)

APPENDIX D

The Incredible Harvest Excursion of 1908

W. J. C. Cherwinski

THE TORONTO *Daily Star* reporter sent down to the city's Union Station in the wee hours of a mid-August day in 1908 witnessed what he considered an awesome sight: "Hundreds of telescope valises with coats strapped to them are stumbling blocks to traffic in the...station. Thousands of small parcels and lunches are falling from the hands of heavily laden excursionists, or are left behind to be remembered later with regrets."[1] His sketch described a scene repeated annually over four decades in a number of railway stations, large and small, in a number of cities and towns across the eastern half of Canada. The event involved the largest mass movement of men organized to meet a specific peacetime need. The crusade for this civilian army was to protect the nation's most valuable commodity from the vagaries of prairie weather. Each August the Canadian Pacific Railway Company (and other companies in later years) organized low-cost harvest excursions to transport to the west able-bodied men, preferably farmers, from the Maritimes and central Canada to help farmers to harvest their crops before winter permanently gripped the region.

It was a crusade because the Wheat Economy was critical to the nation's development. To sustain it Canadians everywhere had been bombarded for years with propaganda about the fantastic opportunities available in the west for people with money or ambition or both. Land was cheap or free for the asking, jobs were plentiful, and wages were high. Granted, there were dangers, largely created by writers of cheap romantic publications, but this only enhanced the sense of adventure.[2] These publicity agents created a myth or mystique about the west which was only partly true even in good times and a total fabrication in bad.

Myths were necessary because the prairies needed people in large numbers. Permanent settlers were most desirable but they, once settled, required skilled help in even larger numbers. One need only scan the numerous "heart rendering appeals for additional help" received by provincial and federal agencies to realize that apart from the weather, an adequate supply of cheap labour was the farmer's single most important problem.[3] While farm labour was needed year round, it was in great demand in spring during seeding and absolutely crucial in autumn during harvest. Other sectors of the prairie economy including mining, ranching, lumbering, and railway construction competed with farmers for labour and to satisfy them the creation of a large floating pool of labour which could be tapped at will in any given year became the main objective.[4] Thus the harvest excursions became an integral part of prairie labour supply.

Besides the cheap labour they might provide, harvest excursions also made solid business sense to all interested parties. The CPR's stake in western Canadian land meant that the company also had a decided interest in prairie prosperity. Especially since a part-time harvester could become a full-time settler who might homestead or even purchase railway land. (In 1906, for example, Immigration Branch officials estimated that 30 per cent of the harvesters stayed.[5]) At the very least he might advertise the bounty of the west to his friends and relations on his return home. Besides, the service the railway provided meant that excursions were inexpensive ventures.

For the three prairie provincial governments as well, harvest excursions, if properly run, were extremely useful politically both in silencing labour-starved farmers and in attracting potential settlers. Consequently Manitoba even sent its own recruiting agent to the Maritimes in some years.[6] Meanwhile Ottawa officials encouraged excursions because they too realized the importance of having high paying jobs available in the autumn when the economy was beginning to slow down.

For the men who journeyed to the west as harvesters, the reasons for going were numerous. An escape from a jilted lover perhaps, or a pre-nuptial last fling, or even the unexpected advent of fatherhood must have figured in some men's decisions.

The younger ones saw it as a chance for freedom at small cost since "papas kept a tight hold on the money." Others took advantage of the opportunity to visit friends or just look around.[7] For the majority, however, the harvest excursion meant either survival or self-improvement. To the largest number it was simply a matter of good, quick money to tide them and their families over a long winter; for some, however, it meant a chance at success in the real land of opportunity.

Whatever their reasons for travelling to the northwest, the excursionists shared a distorted image of the west whose message was that opportunity and success were assured to those who dared to venture forth. As a consequence they were determined to "go west," although often wages at home were comparable and the hours of work were certainly shorter.[8] Since two levels of government and the nation's foremost railway had spent so much time and money creating the myth, they were loath to taint it with the reality of terrible weather, primitive conditions, deadly boredom, and possible failure. In fact, there is evidence to indicate that some highly-placed officials were accomplices in deception by actually conspiring to withhold information which could jeopardize the flow of both settlers and workers.[9]

In the long term perhaps the myth and the means of its propagation may have been justified. It is less easy to condone it in the short term in light of the hardship and widespread personal suffering experienced by the 1908 harvest excursionists in their pursuit of the myth. This paper, which relates the experiences of these excursionists from departure to dispersal across the prairies, is both an examination of what happened on one occasion when myth and reality differed markedly, and simply a good story.

John Thompson's recent study of harvest excursions does place them within the context of the prairie and national economies and therefore much of the detail does not require repeating. Suffice it to say here that as a means of recruiting labour they were unique in North America and a subject of envy to United States agriculture officials.[10] First offered in 1890 when less than 300 men from Ontario travelled west free of charge, their numbers increased rapidly as more western land was settled, their points of origin were expanded, and a basic nominal charge, considerably smaller than a regular fare, was levied by the railway company for the service. By the time Saskatchewan and Alberta became provinces the annual affair appeared to be quite systematic and well organized. Using a method introduced in 1903 each local improvement district provided information on the number of harvesters needed to its provincial department of agriculture which made an estimate of the total required.[11] Then the railway company ran advertisements in every major community newspaper from Toronto east, gradually building up to the announcement of the actual departure dates as determined by harvest forecast experts. The terms were simple. For ten dollars a harvester could buy a ticket to take him from the closest point on the mail line all the way to Winnipeg where he was met by agriculture officials or by farmers' agents and directed to his place of work. If need be, his ticket could be extended 500 miles west to Moose Jaw free of charge. To travel beyond Moose Jaw, but no further than Calgary, MacLeod or Edmonton, or to reach points on branch lines an additional one cent per mile was assessed. Following completion of a minimum of 30 days' labour for one or more farmers, the harvester could, on presentation of his ticket stub, signed by a farmer, return home by regularly scheduled train for another 18 dollars. For Nova Scotians and Prince Edward Islanders the rates were slightly higher. Excursion tickets could also be issued to women. With each ticket the holder could also take 150 pounds of baggage.[12]

Despite the liberal provisions the CPR could not meet the demand and other means to find men had to be found. In 1902 and 1906 the federal Immigration Branch and the railway tried to get harvesters from the Old Country, while at about the same time the two new national railways, the Grand Trunk Pacific and the Canadian Northern, organized their own less extensive excursions.[13] Hence, as Thompson has indicated, the long-term trend was for the number of excursionists to increase as people succumbed to the mystique, but the one in 1908 was exceptional in that it was the first large excursion when 27,500 men were moved, surpassing by 4000 the previous record set in 1906.[14]

A number of factors converged to make excursion organizers anticipate 1908 as a banner year. The acreage put to wheat that spring had been estimated at 20 per cent to 25 per cent higher than 1907 as the number of homesteads settled and the amount of railway and pre-emption land purchased continued to reflect the unbounded optimism associated with the Canadian prairies.[15] While there had been minor changes in agricultural technology over the previous two decades, the process of harvesting the crop was still labour intensive. Horse-drawn reaper binders simplified what previously had been two time-consuming tasks, but the grain still had to dry and harden in stooks of sheaves skillfully constructed to shed rain, a back-breaking job requiring several men for each farm. Depending on the weather, threshing was accomplished several days later by custom crews operating a wheeled threshing machine or separator powered by a twenty-five ton mobile steam-driven engine.

While fewer men were required at this stage the numbers were still considerable. Crews comprised 6 to 50 men working long hours, in some cases several months on end. Consequently, with the increased acreage put to crop each year farmers and officials alike complained that labour shortages were a perennial problem.[16] To compensate, the railways and governments stepped up their campaign to promote the region. This solved the labour problem only temporarily. In the longer term, however, it was exacerbated, for as one provincial official complained:

"Owing to the fact that farmers have, as a rule, been very successful...during recent years, men, who in the older provinces would be content to work under a good master, instead of endeavouring to obtain a farm for themselves, do not long work for wages...but at the earliest opportunity procure a portion of our fertile prairie land and proceed to make homes for themselves."[17]

In 1907 the manpower situation was particularly bad. Poor weather meant a late harvest and farmers were held up for ransom as wages rose dramatically. The CPR even ran an unprecedented "monster" excursion on 12 September to meet the demand for men. It was with memories of this panic situation fresh in their minds that agriculture and railway officials planned for the harvest of 1908.[18] Towards the end of July scattered reports appeared that cutting had begun in some areas indicating that the harvest would be as much as three weeks ahead of 1907. Shortly thereafter the annual game of forecasting the ultimate yield began. This contest, so necessary for the maintenance of the west's reputation, was waged in the nation's press by a variety of public and private "experts" over the next six to eight weeks with one-upmanship as the only recognizable rule. The early consensus in 1908 was that it would be a record crop in the neighbourhood of one hundred and twenty thousand bushels valued at over $85,000,000.[19]

Coincident with the optimistic crop forecast came predictions of a serious scarcity of farm labour. Reports that a good crop in Minnesota and the Dakotas could cut off that traditional though limited source of harvesters from the United States worsened the picture. Manitoba farmers were particularly apprehensive since their experience was that many men chose to go further west into Saskatchewan and Alberta where they would be closer to available homestead lands.[20] Also, remembering 1907, they inundated the offices of the immigration commissioner in Winnipeg, the man responsible for distributing harvesters, demanding assistance. By mid-July, a full month before the harvest would begin, he was processing up to 50 requests per day and within 3 weeks the number of men needed had escalated considerably. The initial provincial totals of estimated requirements at the beginning of August were 12,000 for Manitoba, 10,000 for Saskatchewan, and 2000 for Alberta. Only a very short time later Saskatchewan's projected needs had risen to 20,000 men alone.[21]

The reports of the wages that farmers were willing to pay rose almost as fast. Some were rumoured to be offering as much as $50 per month but a more realistic figure was between $35 and $40 per month or $2.50 per day plus board for an experienced hand, and between $15 and $25 for a greenhorn. It was the daily rate that was of interest to potential excursionists and it was significantly higher than the going rate of $1.50 per day without board for railway construction.[22]

Accounts of the state of the prairie wheat crop, the expected labour shortage, and the wages to be paid to harvesters appeared in a variety of newspapers across the country that summer as a prelude to the first harvest excursion advertisements which were printed in all papers in Ontario and points east after the third week of July. Their very tone indicated urgency as those interested were told by the CPR to "Get Ready" because 30,000 harvesters were needed on the prairies.[23] Later the figure was scaled down to 25,000 but there was still "work for all at good wages." To meet the demand the railway would run specials leaving the Maritimes on 11 August and 5 September and 12 other trains would leave Ontario points between 14 August and

14 September. These ads, which ran daily for two weeks, also gave details of the fares to be paid by prospective harvesters.[24]

Despite the railway company's efforts, predictions still called for a shortage of harvesters. Not much help could be expected from western cities. Although it had been a bad year for urban employment especially in Winnipeg, the *Free Press* concluded that most of the skilled unemployed thought harvest work beneath them. There was even a suggestion that prisoners be paroled for the harvest but that idea was loudly condemned by organized labour.[25]

By early August there was every indication that the publicity and myth-making had not worked. Yet, unpredictably, men from across the country responded to the last-minute appeal for harvesters. Railway construction workers began to leave their jobs, seriously threatening that year's building programme. The national CPR shopworkers' strike which began on 5 August created another unexpected source of help when numerous ancillary workers were laid off. Also unexpectedly, the economy slowed down dramatically in July and scores of urban breadwinners, many without work all summer, saw the harvest as an opportunity to assist their families through a long winter or to create a new life in the west with a small grubstake to get them started.[26]

Early ticket sales in the Maritimes were slow,[27] but by departure time every station on the main line was blocked as branch lines and the Intercolonial funnelled in excursionists from the entire region as rumours spread that there would be a farmers' agent aboard hiring men at rates considerably higher than the year before.[28] There were six trains set to depart the Maritimes on 11 August, each carrying between 9 and 14 cars and up to 2 baggage cars. Each car held 50 persons and by the time all the trains passed through Fredericton Junction, 3500 of the 5200 Maritimers were on board, surpassing all previous records. The CPR had only planned on a total of 4500 with the result that the surplus had to wait for extra cars to be marshalled.[29]

From the beginning the 1908 harvest excursion was marked by misfortune. The first victim was Fred Leman, a young farmer from Hunter River, P.E.I., who was killed when he jumped from the train when it failed to stop at the station at

Kensington.[30] For Islanders on the train the tragedy created some excitement, but for the rest the mind-numbing realities of low-cost transcontinental travel became immediately apparent. The common denominator for all excursionists was another CPR exclusive, the colonist car built to transport large numbers of immigrants to the west which was sparse and functional but offered little by way of comfort. A Toronto *Star* reporter described one of them thus:

"The majority have slat seats, the kind that leave marks. A few have thin cushions. At night the slat seats are pulled out and beds formed in the same way as the ordinary Pullman. But they are not Pullman beds. The passengers carry their own bed linen in the form of quilts and blankets, and there is no porter to tuck them under their chins at night."

In addition each car had a stove for cooking and a supply of water for drinking and washing.[31]

A routine was quickly established by the men despite the few comforts offered and it was broken only by periodic stops to purchase food and other necessities. Almost automatically those with liquor sought and settled in with others similarly fortified and the resulting boisterous behaviour continued unabated. Veterans reunited to reminisce about earlier efforts to tame the west while those venturing forth for the first time listened in awe to their tales.

The trip from Fredericton Junction through Maine and the Eastern Townships provided little diversion from the increasingly painful monotony. At Montreal the trains with a complete complement of coaches continued on the main line to Ottawa while the rest went to Toronto to pick up additional colonist cars. These would rejoin the main line later near Sudbury. Meanwhile additional trains were being marshalled at Toronto to accommodate the 7000 to 8000 expected from Ontario in the first contingent, and there, as in the eastern provinces, the response was greater than anticipated. Twenty-five hundred tickets were sold in Toronto alone on 14 August, and an equal number was expected the next day. Meanwhile, many more were reported to be gathering at points outside the city.[32]

Significantly, of the excursionists leaving Ontario centres, it was estimated that only one-third were farmers. The rest were craftsmen, labourers, and clerks from small towns who saw an opportunity for work or for an inexpensive holiday, or unemployed Toronto labourers who had been "sleeping in lodging houses and living on one meal a day all summer." Also among them were 100 women, some of whom hoped to get work as kitchen assistants on "big Western farms," and some Italian and central European immigrants who wanted to use the excursion as a stepping stone to a homestead.[33] For railway officials the immediate problem was providing space for the numerous people who descended on Union Station and who had to wait, in some cases up to nine hours, to board a train. For the first-time travellers, meanwhile, it meant confusion caused by doubt and apprehension. The result was numerous false alarms as each train that arrived, no matter what its destination, was besieged by "a crowd of bundle-laden excursionists who struggle[d] on, hanging by every available grip" until told of their error whereby "they tumble[d] down dejectedly, and settled down to gather energy to attack the next arrival."[34] To pass the time, most ultimately dipped into their three-day food supply while others preferred the bottle, but an observer noted that the majority were more concerned with protecting their possessions so they remained quiet until they boarded the correct train.[35]

While the southern Ontario excursionists awaited departure, the lead group in the Maritime contingent had already crossed the Ottawa River and was well into the province. By this time the men had become restless, particularly the tipplers whose limited supply of spirits had disappeared. A nasty incident triggered by a minor train wreck at Chalk River on 13 August, however, brought sudden unexpected relief for both the bored and the thirsty.

The Chalk River affair became one of the highlights of the 1908 excursion because of later repercussions. During the hour's delay the men left the train and descended on the local hotel where they threw out the owner when he resisted them and carried off over $1000 worth of liquor and cigars, the cash register containing $300, and a large quantity of beer which replaced the water in the tanks on each car. From this point on any attempt to maintain law and order became futile and the single CPR constable was ignored as the men ranged widely throughout the trains in search of excitement. For those not involved, the next leg of the trip became a terrifying nightmare. Within a short period fighting was reported as general with cuts and bruises wide-spread. Some of the revellers even tried to lynch one excursionist but he was rescued by his friends. Meanwhile, two others were chased off one of the trains when it slowed down.[36]

Each stop brought incidents of looting of a degree "that would bring discredit to a colonial regiment," forcing merchants in each town to lock their premises. The excursionists on the next train simply forced the doors and openly walked away with what they wanted. At Mackey's Station they even raided the home of the station agent and demolished the furniture, while in another community they reportedly drank three taverns dry during a few minutes' stopover.

Further on the men "swarmed out" and raided the garden tended by two sisters, and when the women protested the hungry raiders pelted them with onions.[37] At one station, however, a woman answered insults directed at her by shooting at the train and a man from Merigomish, Nova Scotia, received a crease in the head as a memento. Forewarned by telegram, a specially re-inforced North Bay police contingent met the first train and promptly arrested seven men for "attempted hooliganism," but they were released and allowed to return to the train as soon as it was ready to depart.[38]

Back on the train the "drink-crazed brutes" continued their rampage. Some even brought out the firearms they were carrying and as one of the trains passed through a deep cut they shot at an Indian sitting on an embankment. She escaped, but a horse at another place was not as lucky. Others threw bottles at the section men working on the line, causing several to be hospitalized for cuts and gashes. When there was nothing of interest outside the train, they turned their attention to the interior where they broke windows, smashed chandeliers, splintered shutters and left the coaches in a "disgracefully dirty" condition.[39]

With the rowdies in control of the train those who simply wanted to be left alone were "...forced to seek refuge in certain cars from which the others were excluded." Some tried to intervene when things got out of hand, but this only led to "worse trouble" and they were forced to retreat. The few women on one of the trains were herded into a single car, but this ploy offered little protection as several rapes were reported by observers, and one Maritime school teacher allegedly was stripped and assaulted repeatedly.[40] One woman, travelling from Halifax to meet her husband in Edmonton, was so distressed that she collapsed.[41]

Momentary order was restored when the trains reached Fort William on 14 August. There Lewis Cuttle, a one-armed, 50 year old harvester from Truro was arrested for having Chalk River Hotel liquor in his possession and another man was led away for breaking a glass door on the train. Once under way again, however, the shouting and singing continued as did the intimidation of the other passengers.

West of the lakehead the Maritimers discovered another source of entertainment. The CPR was constructing another track parallel to the main line from Fort William to Winnipeg that summer using Italian and Doukhobor labourers and the harvesters on the first train directed "an indiscriminate fusillade of empty cans, bottles and other unnecessary articles" toward these foreigners. The later trains, and particularly the last one in the first contingent with several Ontario coaches attached to it, felt the full impact of this act. Under cover of darkness the construction labourers retaliated with rocks hurled at the windows of the train. One man was struck in the face and knocked out, while another received a scalp wound from what was reported to be a Winchester bullet. Soon every window was smashed forcing the faint of heart to seek refuge in the upper berths, while the rest replied in kind with every possible missile they could muster. Revolvers that had been kept for future contingencies were brought out to defend the train. On meeting a group of Italians east of Kenora, a harvester threw a heavy bottle into the crowd killing one man, while one was shot in the shoulder and another in the hand. While this incident ended the serious injuries, the train still was forced "to run a continuous gauntlet over the entire division" until it reached Winnipeg in the early hours of 15 August.[42] For the meek a four and half day ordeal was over.

A new reporter on hand to see the arrival of the first train commented that "a more disreputable looking aggregation [had] never pulled into the CPR depot." Using a comparison popular at the time he claimed that:

"No party of Galician immigrants ever had such disreputable appearances as these tenderfeet, who started out West with the idea that they were going to be bad men, and arrived here, some without hats, or coats, others with blood-besprinkled shirts, and clothes, and many of them with black eyes and bruised faces, which had not been washed since they left the East."[43]

Accompanying him to greet the "embryo desperadoes" was a squad of police armed with descriptions of the alleged law breakers. Of these, two men, both Nova Scotians, were arrested for willfully damaging railway property and promptly sent to join the two captured in Fort William to face trial. The remainder evaded arrest.[44] Police also cordoned off the last train when it arrived later in an effort to find the killer of the Italian labourer, but he too escaped custody.[45] As a precaution railway officials locked the waiting room in the depot and prepared the basement for the men when they detrained. At that moment making trouble was the farthest thing from anyone's mind, however, and once released they cheered at the termination of a long and arduous journey.

Long before the first contingent of the 1908 harvest excursion arrived in Winnipeg detailed accounts of the escapades of its members were telegraphed from coast to coast and appeared in all the major papers. Journalistic comment was quick and scathing, most of it leveled at the Maritimers. The *Free Press* conceded that every year excursionists "cast off the restraints and decencies of civilization as they find themselves headed for the West" and stimulated by drink their behaviour deteriorated into "brutal hooliganism," but 1908's bunch was simply "drunken savagery running amuck." It recommended that all the law-breakers be jailed. Both the railway and the Ontario government were blamed for not taking adequate preventative measures and for not arresting the guilty earlier. In the editor's opinion, the only reason the "riotousness" was not carried into Manitoba was because the participants were too worn out and battered.[46] The *Toronto Daily Star* pointed the finger at the same people, although it did concede that the Maritimers were decent citizens in their own communities who had been affected by "distance from home, the excitement of unusual travel, and the leadership of a few naturally inclined to rowdyism."[47]

The discussion was not confined entirely to the editorial pages. James Hartery, the Manitoba agent responsible for the excursionists, confirmed that the rowdies were "almost entirely"

Maritimers who from "the first time they went to the west... raised a commotion and their successors each year considered it their duty to live up to the tradition."[48] The Fredericton *Daily Gleaner*, by proudly announcing that "Our Harvesters Raise Big Riot" in its headline on the Chalk River raid story, agreed that their behaviour was not completely unexpected.[49] A former Maritime excursionist residing in Winnipeg gave one clue as to the reason, when he pointed out that despite their respectable backgrounds "upon their return they are afflicted with a desire to spin horrible tales of the wildness and wooliness of the west and their exploits." These yarns, while largely imaginary, "fire the blood of the younger boys and when they come west in a few years they set out to eclipse all previous records," led by "some reckless daredevils who do anything in the way of rowdyism." Consequently they became a disgrace to their families and their region.[50]

The only unqualified defender of the excursionists was "Islander" writing to the *Free Press*. He claimed that the reports were deliberately exaggerated to discredit the Maritimes and "to give an entirely wrong impression of the best settlers Western Canada is getting." In his opinion the theft of beer from the Chalk River Hotel was justified since the CPR had failed to provide an adequate supply of water to the cars.[51] But whether the behaviour of the harvesters was warranted or not, the 1908 excursion was generally judged by commentators as the worst ever.

The reports of lawlessness on the trains had almost immediate consequences. The first to feel the pinch was the CPR as land-seekers from Ontario who planned to travel west with their wives began to have second thoughts. Pressure from ticket agents forced the railway to hire 20 special constables within days, arm them with batons and revolvers and instruct them in crowd control. Consequently no further trouble was experienced on subsequent trains and the 2500 harvesters that arrived on 22 August were described as "respectable and quiet" and "...of the kind that is required to do the work in this part of the country."[52] Meanwhile, attempts by the railway company to track down the perpetrators of the "disgraceful outrage" against the women on the first train produced no results, largely because, as the company weakly explained, it took place east of Fort William and therefore out of the jurisdiction of Winnipeg authorities.[53]

THE HARVEST TRAIN

While CPR officials were trying desperately to deflect criticism over the behaviour of the Maritime excursionists, they faced the more pressing problem of getting these men distributed to places where they were needed. For some of the experienced harvesters it was a simple matter owing to commitments based on contacts made in previous years. A few others were hired by farmers or their agents standing on the station platform in Winnipeg. Some harvesters had engagements further west on the main line and for them it was simply a matter of waiting for the right train. They were the exception, however. Most did not know where to go and simply wanted to try their luck elsewhere: for the company this meant trying to accommodate them without interfering with regular train service. A special building was set aside and extra ticket agents and baggage handlers provided to avoid congestion in the main waiting room. In addition the building was fenced in to control the crowds and trains were rescheduled to minimize difficulties.[54]

Despite the precautions the CPR distribution system at Winnipeg broke down almost immediately. Some of the Maritimers did go west in coaches attached to regular trains, but most were forced to wait more than a day while their eight cars of baggage were stored in a private warehouse. While they remained in Winnipeg the depot processed a record 20,000 passengers on the evening of 16 August, half of whom were other excursionists. Meanwhile, 11 more harvester trains from Ontario with 120 coaches were approaching to Winnipeg, and 4 more trains had not yet departed.[55]

It was only after the congestion created on 16 August had been cleared up that a special train of 20 coaches was made up to leave for the west at midnight. The interminable hours of waiting resulted in pandemonium when the boarding announcement was made and the gates were opened. The *Free Press* reported that:

"...Spectators were given a sample of that mob spirit which has rendered some of the excursion trains beyond control. The men fought and crowded and pushed with all their might to force their way by main strength through the narrow opening, and when this was accomplished amid much swearing and wrecking of baggage and clothing, they ran toward the cars like a lot of insane men, shouting at the top of their voices. Women who were endeavouring to board the cars were forced back by the stampede, and the men climbed aboard through the doorways and windows as though they were being pursued."[56]

A number of harvesters did not catch the west-bound special and had to settle back, along with those who arrived after them, to await another train. This alternative was not only wearisome but expensive as their limited subsistence funds rapidly dwindled. As some began to wander around the city, several burglaries took place which the press promptly "attributed to undesirable visitors from the east." In one instance a man walked into a store on Portage Avenue and held up a cashier with a revolver and escaped, while around the same time a number of residences were entered and money and property stolen.[57]

Most of the harvesters eventually returned to the stockade to sleep and wait and by morning of 18 August the atmosphere was tense, the mood ugly, and officials apprehensive. At 10:30 the first disturbance took place, allegedly started by one George Ryall. The depot master tried to subdue him but he resisted and the CPR police removed him from the building only to be met by over 1000 men who converged to prevent his arrest. He was pulled off a police wagon but the driver retrieved his prisoner by whipping the crowd "with the greatest vigor and enthusiasm" and delivered him to the police station.[58]

Another incident two days later involved almost identical circumstances. This time James Forrester of Truro was "spoken to" for "acting in an indecent manner" in the depot. When he persisted he was thrown out by railway police and arrested by a city constable. His friends, seeing his plight, rushed the policeman shouting "rescue, rescue." Four extra officers arrived and after a lengthy tussle with some of the mob, estimated at 1500, Forrester was subdued with a truncheon and thrown into the police rig. His would-be rescuers gathered around the police station for awhile but finally dispersed. In the meantime the CPR locked the depot and assigned special constables to prevent a recurrence of trouble.[59] The long hours of waiting had had their effect on all concerned.

With so much bored and bitter humanity plaguing Winnipeg, the primary concern of the CPR and municipal officials was to dispose of them somewhere before the tense situation escalated into something even more serious. The railway assured the men that they were badly needed on branch lines in Manitoba and eastern Saskatchewan. Most excursionists were reluctant to venture off the man line, however, and to some extent their hesitation was justified. Many had been told that they would receive at least $45 per month but this rate was not being offered in Manitoba. Naturally, they assumed that it applied further west.[60] Moreover, since most were unfamiliar with the country, they were loath to detrain only to find themselves stranded if they were not hired immediately at satisfactory wages, a sentiment shared by those who feared being separated from their luggage stored in the baggage car. In addition, some harvesters heard that a special had been dispatched which missed all the connections with the branch lines and this must have convinced them to go as far as their tickets would take them.[61]

Some excursionists, of course, took the railway's advice and tried their luck in small communities, but their initial experiences proved disappointing. For those stuck in Manitoba points the problem was that both the railway company and the Manitoba provincial immigration officers, unbeknownst to each other, had sent batches of men to the same places. Consequently, at Deloraine, in the southwest corner of the province 100 harvesters were reported to be dependent on the resources of the town, a situation similar to the one being experienced by Virden on the main line.[62] Meanwhile, at Indian Head, 300 miles west of Winnipeg, 24 harvesters were hanging around on 22 August waiting for cutting to begin. There they made the town "a busy and interesting place" by holding nightly concerts in the hall which served as their home. Within a week the number had swollen to 100, and then to over 200 by which time all semblance of fun had disappeared for the men and the community. Bitter complaints were directed at the CPR and residents feared trouble if the situation did not improve quickly. The following letter, one of many received by the *Globe* from stranded farm labourers appealing to others to stay home, sums up their collective frustration:

"In every town and village in the country dozens of men are walking around without a cent to their names, and practically starving. They are all willing to work, but there is no work to do. These same railways that enticed them to come out here by their false representations now refuse to carry them back to the East at the reduced rate, taking refuge behind and basing their argument upon the fact that the men must first put in a month on the farm, a condition that the railway companies knew when they were flooding the country with these men would not, and could not be fulfilled."[63]

While the plight of farm workers stranded in small villages and towns gave cause for concern, they at least were relatively comfortable compared to those who rode the trains all the way to Moose Jaw where the next major episode in the tragicomedy of the 1908 harvest excursion unfolded. One hundred and fifty men, "some...evidently...from the happy bunch which made such a triumphant journey through New Ontario," arrived there on 16 August, many still bearing "the signs of battle." There was some initial reluctance to hire them because of the news reports of their rowdy reputations, but the local Board of Trade took the responsibility for distributing them and they were dispersed quickly to local farmers or down the Soo Line to the southeast of the city.[64]

The real flood began on 17 August. One hundred harvesters arrived that day and two more large groups were expected on the next. Even at this early date local officials agreed that no more men were needed for at least a week and a half until the threshing started. Moreover, it was expected that the farmers would do more than the usual amount of work themselves, because the season was early and the crop had only short and medium straw which required less effort.[65]

Nevertheless the CPR kept bringing harvesters into the city. By 20 August the surplus had turned into a glut and the municipal government found itself feeding 200 individuals who had no visible means of support. The Board of Trade dispatched some of them down the Soo Line that evening and the CPR offered others jobs laying track south of the city. Local farmers hired a few more while those who acquired some money bought tickets to Alberta, but altogether they made little impression on the total and by 24 August hundreds of men were still walking the streets and sleeping in the trains or on the floor of the YMCA.[66]

The situation in Moose Jaw became even more critical later in the month when numerous men arrived intent on getting one of the homesteads that were to be distributed from the local Land Office. As a consequence, the land rush and the excursions together placed a tremendous strain on the resources of the small community of about 9000 people and accommodation of any kind was impossible to find.

Another problem which the city faced was a marked increase of petty crime and disorderly conduct. As the Moose Jaw *Times* observed, there seemed "to be a rather tough lot of men about town with nothing to do except get drunk." Since the land seekers were an "orderly lot" the paper concluded that the "toughs" were the "off-scourings of eastern cities who came out with the harvesters." In one instance four men were discovered in a car in the stockyards consuming a case of liquor stolen from a local warehouse. One of them was reportedly so drunk that he was oblivious of a broken leg. In response the local judge cracked down on the "crime wave" by meting out justice swiftly in all cases and the city's cells were filled to overflowing most of the time.[67]

The growing sense of apprehension felt by the community was exacerbated by increased hostility expressed by the harvesters themselves for the helplessness of their position. Without money or even a place to sleep most of them directed criticism at the CPR. Publicly the railway replied that the reports of stranded harvesters were exaggerated and they "...referred to men who did not particularly want to work, or who were dissatisfied with the conditions offered them." The *Free Press'* crop expert, P. M. Robinson, shared this view. While on tour of the prairies he found that the unemployed hanging around Moose Jaw were "...young fellows, who came from the city of Toronto, look unfit for harvest work, and being homesick, are looking for a cheap trip back."[68] Yet the CPR considered them fit for railway construction labour and almost immediately offered either track work at $1.75 per day or a free trip down the Soo Line. Sixty took the first option and over a hundred the second, giving Moose Jaw a brief breathing spell.

Despite the railway company's efforts the harvesters considered the job offer a betrayal of the original deal. On 24 August, for example, one individual, possibly an IWW spokesman, set up a box at a major intersection and harangued the 100 or so men gathered around him. Shouting that they "had been wronged and misled" by the CPR's advertising extolling the bounties of the west, he urged them to do something. A YMCA secretary defused the situation before it got out of hand by admitting that conditions were bad. He assured the men that even though the city was not responsible for the sad state of affairs and had warned the harvesters to stay away, it would do all it could for them. He personally offered the YMCA as a place to sleep but only to those who arrived that day and not to those who refused the railway's offer. By nightfall nearly 200 more had departed Moose Jaw. It made no difference, however, for 3 more trains had arrived and disgorged another 500 men. While they were, according to the *Times*, of a "better class" than the Maritimers and had some money, they still had no place to stay and were forced to seek shelter where they could.[69]

With the continuing influx of farm workers the situation became so serious that the Saskatchewan government intervened to protect the province's reputation and thereby its future supply of harvesters. Its Department of Agriculture requested the railway to inform those still on trains east of Winnipeg where help was required. When still more men arrived in Moose Jaw, direct consultation took place with Winnipeg officials who gave assurance that no more would be sent on to Moose Jaw. Yet, incredibly, another three trains pulled into the community soon after "for some reason or other, perhaps because it was not known where to send the men."[70] Since the city could not afford to feed so many, agriculture officials again approached the railway company for other solutions and won the assurance that the harvesters could return east for $18 without putting in the requisite 30 days work. However, they soon discovered that this was no solution because few had the money and those who did wanted to stay until threshing began when they knew they could get work for at least six to eight weeks.[71]

In total, Moose Jaw had to cope with 5500 harvesters during fall 1908. The problem of unemployed farm workers was by no means confined to that city, however. Saskatoon, for example, reluctantly received 1260 men via the CPR branch line and the CNR main line which connected it to Winnipeg. There the Board of Trade also took it upon itself to distribute them, but in a ten day period filled only a dozen requests from local farmers; the rest were placed digging city sewers or helping on railway construction in the area, rather demeaning options for men who had come west to make "big money" harvesting.[72]

Meanwhile Regina, as the capital and the province's largest

city, faced special problems because it became the final refuge for the many harvesters who met failure elsewhere. A particularly pathetic story involved 12 men from the first contingent who had bought tickets down the Soo Line from Moose Jaw only to find no work. They trudged back to Moose Jaw, where they too fell on the mercy of the Board of Trade. They remained two days and then set out to find government work in Regina. The two meals they received before leaving turned out to be their last for three days: what they obtained in addition they did by their collective wits, and in some instances they were not very successful. At Belle Plain, half-way to their destination, for example, they begged for food from a man who said he was a parson and offered to help them, but after a two-hour wait they approached the house only to find him beating his wife in a drunken rage. As a result the men bartered extra pairs of pants for food.

These "sturdy sons of the soil who never before had known what it was to be without food"[73] were somewhat the worse for wear when they joined close to 200 others in like circumstances at the CPR depot in the capital. Without 50 cents among them and with no immediate prospects for improvement the larger group had earlier held an "indignation meeting" on 23 August where they condemned the railway for not sending them back home and accused the company of misrepresentation, and as one observer noted, "...it would have required but little to have incited them to open revolt."[74] Fearing serious trouble the Salvation Army stepped in immediately and gave them temporary bed and board and no doubt spiritual solace. The Regina City Council took longer to act but after 24 August it fed the men two meals a day at City Hall. In the meantime the mayor and one councillor demanded that the CPR and the government find work for the men or ship them back. The Agriculture Department appealed in turn to all the railway companies to drop the 30 day work rule and to provide work for the men.[75]

With pressure building from all directions the CPR offered work for 200 at $1.75 per day and agreed to transport them to the job site east of Winnipeg. After 60 days work they could return home for the $18 excursionists' fare. The Canadian Northern, which needed 100 men to ballast the Regina to Brandon line, offered the same terms. In addition all carriers cancelled later excursion trains thus forestalling further complications.[76]

Appendix D: The Harvest Excursion of 1908

In spite of the grudging attempts by the railway companies to make amends, the stranded harvesters were far from ecstatic. Many had left what they claimed were good jobs in the east—paying $2 per day in some cases—to earn more money. Understandably, the railway offer was a blow since out of wages they had to pay $4.50 per week board, $1.25 per month medical fees, and another $2.50 per month for blanket rental. With no bargaining power whatsoever they were forced to "acquiesce to this proposal." Yet when they presented themselves at the depot at the appointed time they found no one there from either company to take them to the job site. The situation was cleared up eventually but not to anyone's satisfaction.[77]

The harvesters who were able to wait for the start of threshing fared substantially better than those forced into railway work. Before long all the surplus labour was absorbed and the prairies experienced another shortage of men. Once employed all the men disappeared from public record and most of their follow-up experiences have been lost. Some obviously fulfilled their desires and returned home happy. Others must have stayed because circumstances left them with insufficient funds to get home. They drifted to the cities in search of work and there became a burden on municipal ratepayers causing civic officials to voice repeated opposition to harvest excursions in later years. Yet others who had used the excursions as a means of introduction to the west and its riches returned to the east disillusioned.[78]

The harvest excursion of 1908 had been a disappointment for large numbers of workers. The tales of their hardships discouraged harvesters the following year. Only 18,246 came in 1909 and the prairie provinces had an extremely difficult time procuring men. As the Saskatchewan Department of Agriculture noted in its report for that year, "...short of using compulsion, nothing...could be done to induce men to answer the call of the western harvest fields."[79] But memories were short and in later years new records were set as the expanding wheat economy absorbed more and more men with a pre-war high of 57,000 journeying west in 1912.[80] Like their predecessors, they flocked to the large centres almost by instinct creating the same problems as before.

While the human factor still caused chaos especially when

supply and demand markedly diverged, there is no doubt that the agencies involved in recruiting and distributing harvest labour learned more from the 1908 experiences than the men. Harvest help was treated somewhat less as commodity and more as a component necessary to the continued prosperity of the prairie economy with the result that greater care was taken to properly direct the men wherever they gathered.[81] Also, the CPR imposed a half-cent per mile charge beyond Winnipeg to discourage the invasion of Moose Jaw. Provincial governments took measures to decrease their dependence on eastern harvesters by recruiting farm help from prairie cities and even by using public servants when the situation was particularly bad.[82] Yet the circumstances surrounding the 1908 harvest excursion revealed flaws in the system of recruitment and distribution of temporary farm help so serious that minor modifications and adjustments could not possibly have solved them.

The major problem in 1908 was that the provincial governments and the railways had planned badly. The former, afraid of not getting enough harvesters in time, overestimated requirements. The latter made little effort to spread out the trains more effectively with weekly quotas to avoid congestion at Winnipeg and Moose Jaw. Also basic to the problem of planning was the system of crop forecasting by which manpower requirements were determined.

Saskatchewan's Deputy Commissioner of Agriculture predicted difficulties as early as 1905 when he complained of "the absurd estimates or rather guesses, made by irresponsible and ill-informed people and given undue publicity through the press.... It need scarcely be pointed out that the immense agricultural development of the province, which is now taking place demands a correlative expansion on the part of the crop reporting and statistical service."[83]

Still another component in predicting harvest needs was the amount of land being homesteaded. The estimators neglected to consider the "phenomenal" number of homesteaders who had arrived over the previous year, especially in the area west of Saskatoon, and whose land had no crop and who were themselves "...only too glad to get a little work to help them over the winter."[84] They also ignored the recent arrival of numerous settlers from central Europe who pursued subsistence agriculture using large families to meet labour requirements thereby indirectly contributing to the surplus.

The 1908 situation also involved circumstances which were beyond the capacity of even the most perceptive planner. For example, there is no doubt that the economic picture in the summer of that year, and the CPR strike contributed to the unusual demand for excursion tickets. In addition, these circumstances spawned a new kind of excursionist who was more likely to be an unemployed city worker who in desperation boarded the first advertised trains to come along, whether at Fredericton Junction or Toronto, rather than an Ontario or Maritime farmer who waited until the local harvest was over before catching one of the excursions scheduled in early September to coincide with western threshing. Moreover, this early rush of first-timers contributed not only to the glut at Winnipeg but also to the large number who insisted on ignoring advice by continuing on as far as their tickets would take them. Once in the west they had to compete with an unexpected influx of local urban labour and harvesters from the western United States.[85]

The prairie climate was another unpredictable quantity which cannot be overlooked in connection with the 1908 fiasco. Manpower estimates had been based on an early and heavy crop, but a dry spell and an early frost cut the yield to almost half. Not only did this make farmers more cost-conscious in the binding and stooking stage but it also meant a shorter threshing season. Both factors thus contributed to the harvesters' difficulties.[86]

The failure to recognize the prairie climate's destructive potential, the inflated crop forecasts, the manpower requirements based on these predictions and the kind of harvester who was attracted to the west that year share a common element which helps to explain the problems experienced by all those concerned with the 1908 excursion. This was the myth that Canada's garden was the key to the nation's growth, continued prosperity, and in times of stress its salvation. Canadians believed the myth which had been propagated with so much effort. In times of prosperity the surplus labour requirements were left to the immigrants to fill, but with the slump in the economy in mid-summer a substantially larger number decided to exercise the option to which they felt entitled as Canadians, and they "...instinctively look[ed] westward in hope of better things."[87] The immigrants laying track east of Winnipeg were not Canadian and the harvesters did not consider them eligible to partake of the fruits of the garden at such times of difficulty and they were treated accordingly. Some of the harvesters also showed by their behaviour that they believed the west to be untamed wilderness where they could shed the restraints of civilized society. This part of the myth was exploded by railway police and municipal constables intent on maintaining law and order. More important, the fruits of the west were found to consist of interminable waits in crowded railway stations, soup lines, uncomfortable benches and YMCA floors, and sometimes demeaning work at very low wages. For those who did find sufficient work early the reality was not less appealing than the myth; for the unfortunate the mystique of the west was shattered and with it the unfounded belief in the ability of the nation to provide for all in equal measure.

Some Cape Bretoners who went on the harvest excursion settled permanently in the West. This photo, taken in Alberta in 1912 or 1913, shows (left to right) Andrew Smith, William Wright and John Robert Smith. The Smiths were brothers from Hillsborough, while their first cousin, William, was from Mull River, Inverness County. *(Courtesy Mabou Gaelic and Historical Society)*

Footnotes

Chapter 1
SOME WILD AND WOOLLY TIMES

1 John Herd Thompson, "Bringing in the Sheaves: The Harvest Excursionists, 1890-1929," *Canadian Historical Review*, LIX, 4, 1978, p. 474.

2 E. M. Deyarmond, *Leaves from the Whip Handle Tree* (1974), pp. 21, 22.

3 Lee Zinck, *The Rooster Crows at Dawn* (Hantsport, 1987), pp. 54, 55. But there were no return tickets sold for the excursion!

4 Dr. W. A. Bigelow, *Forceps, Fin and Feather* (Altoona, n.d. but circa 1970), pp. 3, 4.

5 W. J. C. Cherwinski, "The Incredible Harvest Excursion of 1908," *Labour/Le Travailleur*, 5 (Spring 1980), pp. 65-68. See Appendix D, pages 133-156, for Cherwinski's entire article.

6 *Ibid.*, pp. 73-77.

7 Maggie Grant, "The Harvest Excursions," *The Canadian Magazine*, April 30, 1966, p. 7.

8 File G697-1 (1940), CNR, Assistance to...on Harvesters' Excursions. RCMP Historical Section, Ottawa. W. A. Kingsland, General Manager, CNR Eastern Lines, Montreal, to Commissioner Perry, August 19, 1921.

9 W. J. C. Cherwinski, *op. cit.*, p. 70.

10 File G697-1, CNR, RCMP assistance to...H. H. Ward, Deputy Minister of Labour to Commissioner of the RCMP Ottawa, August 17, 1926.

Chapter 2
WHY WERE MARITIMERS WANTED IN THE WEST?

1 One American railroad operated a harvest excursion. *Harper's Magazine* printed an advertisement for such excursions to Minnesota, Dakota, and Montana via the St. Paul, Minneapolis and Manitoba Railway. No date is visible, but the name of A. M. Manvel appears as General Manager of the railway. He was G.M. of the line from 1886 to 1889, and the ad would have appeared during this time. See Freeman Hubbard's article on J. J. Hill, *Railroad Magazine*, December 1978. See also, Albro Martin, *J. J. Hill and the Opening of the Northwest*, pp. 290, 379.

2 A great expansion in sales of gasoline tractors occurred between 1925 and 1930. See Robert E. Ankli, H. Dan Helsberg, and John Herd Thompson, "The Adoption of the Gasoline Tractor in Western Canada," *Canadian Papers in Rural History*, vol. 11 (Gananoque, 1980), pp. 12-35.

3 W. Kaye Lamb, *History of the Canadian Pacific Railway* (New York, 1977), p. 314.

4 *Ibid.*, p. 318.

5 John Herd Thompson, in "Bringing in the Sheaves...," p. 470, says the ticket home could be a fare "equal to that he had paid coming out." However, George V. Haythorne estimates excursion fares to be often less than 25 per cent of regular fare. In 1926 fare on the excursion from

Maritime points to Winnipeg was approximately twenty dollars. Return fare was about twenty-five dollars. George V. Haythorne, "The Harvest Labour Problem in the Canadian Prairie Provinces." Typescript in my possession. This paper, with slight alterations, was published in *Quarterly Journal of Economics*, 1933, pp. 533-544.

6 *Sessional Papers, Canada, Dept. of Agriculture & Immigration*, 1900, p. 352. *Ibid.*, 1905, p. 39. John Herd Thompson gives higher figures for the total number of harvesters in those years.

7 John Herd Thompson, *op. cit.*, p. 487.

8 *Halifax Herald*, December 19, 1948. Thanks to Fred J. MacDonald, Glencoe, and Larry Loomer for bringing this to my attention.

9 Marjorie MacKenzie Hawkins, "My Trip to the West" (typescript). Thanks to John MacQuarrie, Pugwash.

10 John Herd Thompson, "Permanently Wasteful but Immediately Profitable: Prairie Agriculture and the Great War," Canadian Historical Association *Historical Papers*, 1976, p. 195.

11 John Herd Thompson, "Bringing in the Sheaves...," p. 489. Within this passage, Thompson is quoting from AS, UFSCC Papers, Edwards to W. M. Thrasher, 13 Sept. 1928, IX file 146(2).

12 *Ibid.*, p. 471. Within, Thompson quotes from Glenbow, Robert Trussler Collection, "Account of Trip West as Excursioner in 1925." See also "Why Boys and Girls Leave the Farm" in *Canadian Thresherman and Farmer*, Aug. 1908, 38-9.

13 Georgina Binnie Clark, *Wheat and Woman* (Toronto, 1979).

Chapter 3
ABOARD THE TRAINS

1 Quoted in Cherwinski, *op. cit.*, p. 65.

2 Gay Lepkey and Brian West, *Canadian National Railways Passenger Equipment 1867-1992* (Ottawa, 1995), pp. 58, 62, 176-177, 222-223.

3 In a footnote, John Herd Thompson writes: "There are no statistics available on the percentage of Canadian excursionists placed through these services, but in a 1924 study conducted in the American wheat belt, where similar state and federal agencies existed, only 17 per cent of farmers interviewed used these services to obtain their harvesters." Thompson, *op. cit.*, p. 477, fn. 38.

4 George V. Haythorne, *op. cit.* Data from the Department of Labour, Ottawa, for the table on page 16. The figure for Maritime harvesters is in *Sessional Papers. No. 6. Dept. of Agriculture and Immigration Report*, 1902, p. 331.

5 *Sessional Papers. Dept. of Agriculture and Immigration Report*, 1908, p. 554; 1909, pp. 62-63, 1910, p. 226.

6 *Ibid.*, 1902, p. 293. Violent resentment had built up in British Columbia against the 2000 Japanese workers there. See Irving Abella and David Millar, *The Canadian Worker in the Twentieth Century* (Toronto, 1978), p. 26. However, the colour bar did not apply to some kinds of enterprise. Some harvesters may have discovered this on weekend forays in Saskatoon. That prairie city offered visitors to the red-light district a choice of playmates by colour: one of its houses was inhabited exclusively by white whores, a second was all black, and a third was completely Japanese. A similar variety was available in Calgary near the Post Office. In Lethbridge the "Yellow Peril" girls were in old broth-

Footnotes

els along the Belly River. See J. H. Gray, *Red Lights on the Prairies* (Toronto, 1971), pp. 91, 92, 132, 166, 167.

7 H. M. Troper, "The Creek Negroes of Oklahoma and Canadian Immigration 1909-11," *Canadian Historical Review*, 1972, p. 279.

8 *The Pictou Advocate*, August 9, 1901.

9 D. N. Brodie, "The Harvest Excursion," *Glace Bay Mirror*, July 1953.

10 File G687-1. (194). RCMP Assistance to Harvest Trains; RCMP memo to President of the Privy Council, September 9, 1921.

11 Report of RCMP Commissioner, 1924.

12 C. W. Harvison, *The Horsemen* (Toronto, 1967), pp. 9, 10.

13 *Ibid.*, pp. 56, 57.

14 Jim Gowen, Halifax, April 29, 1980.

15 New Glasgow, *Eastern Chronicle*, September 17, 1920.

16 *Ibid.*, September 21, 1920.

17 Frank Parker Day Papers, C109, Dalhousie University Archives, Halifax. F. P. Day to Mabel Day, Winnipeg, August 18, 1920.

18 *Ibid.* For R. L. S., see Leslie Stephen (ed.) *Robert Louis Stevenson, Essays and Reviews* (New York, 1906), pp. 30-56.

19 J. H. Gray, *op. cit.*, pp. 38, 39.

Chapter 5
FINDING WORK: TEACHERS AND FARMHANDS

1 *Canadian Annual Review*, 1906, p. 387; 1904, p. 578.

2 Chester Martin, *"Dominion Lands" Policy* (Toronto, 1973), Chapter 6. Sections eleven and twenty-nine in every surveyed township in the Northwest were set aside as an endowment for the purposes of education. The policy was followed astutely of selling the school lands at high prices. In Saskatchewan the gross proceeds of school land sales amounted to more than 35 million dollars by 1930. Net proceeds to the three Prairie Provinces amounted to over 67 million dollars.

In 1913 Maritime spokesmen attempted to claim compensation for the school lands, citing them as an example of the favourable treatment granted western provinces while the Maritimes were neglected. Premier Matheson of Prince Edward Island summed up the Maritime case: "...these Provinces had to bear a heavy burden of developing the West, partly by their money, but more by their men. I remember being in the West when it was a wilderness and when the conditions in the East were much more favourable. The son has been made better off than the father."

See F. L. Driscoll in Francis W. P. Bolger (ed.), *Canada's Smallest Province* (Charlottetown, 1973), pp. 272-273.

3 Barry Broadfoot, *The Pioneer Years* (Don Mills, 1978), pp. 293-301.

4 Maurice "Blue" MacDonald, Main Street, Glace Bay.

5 Margaret Davidson (ed.), *I Came from Pictou County* (Regina, 1976), pp. 25-26. See Appendix B, pages 118-126, for excerpts from this memoir by Jane MacKay Rutherford.

6 Dr. W. O. Chestnutt, Hartland, N. B., to A. A. MacKenzie, August 4, 1976.

7 John Annesley, "In Canada's Wheat Fields," *The Canadian Countryman*, Oct. 16, 1937. Annesley was from Ontario, or at least had a job there.

8 R. D. Symons, *Many Trails* (Don Mills, 1970), p. 117.

9 *Bluenose Magazine*, Summer 1978.
10 *Coastal Courier*, Glace Bay, March 26, 1980.
11 Lorne Robson, Ronkonkoma, New York to A. A. MacKenzie, 1977.
12 D. N. Brodie, *op. cit.*
13 D. J. Campbell, *Young Nova Scotians at Manitoban Harvest* (New Glasgow, 1908), pp. 9, 12, 13. Thanks to Ken Donovan for this gem.
14 Gerald Friesen, *The Canadian Prairies: A History* (Toronto, 1987), p. 331. The paragraph in which this reference occurs is one of the exceedingly rare occasions when the harvest excursion is even mentioned in any regional or provincial history of the prairies.
15 E. M. Deyarmond, *op. cit.*, p. 97.
16 Robert J. C. Stead, *Grain* (Toronto, 1969), pp. 109, 110.
17 R. L. Yates, *When I Was a Harvester* (New York, 1930), pp. 8, 9.
18 John Herd Thompson's excellent description of the work of stooking and threshing is from "Bringing in the Sheaves...," *op. cit.*, pp. 477-480.
19 *Ibid.* Quote is from Yates, *When I Was a Harvester*, p. 47.
20 *Ibid.* From Kezar interview.
21 *Ibid.* From Walter Wiggins, "Hired man in Saskatchewan," *Marxist Quarterly*, winter 1964, pp. 82-84.
22 *Ibid.* Thompson adds: Some farmers stacked their grain before they threshed it to provide it with more protection from the elements. If a threshing machine was available, however, most Prairie grain growers threshed directly from the stook. By 1907 this technique had become almost universal and by 1915 a farmer who stacked was something of a curiosity. See "Threshing from Stook vs. Stacking," *Canadian Thresherman*, Aug. 1907, pp. 28-33; *Farmer's Advocate*, 9 Sept. 1915; Edward West, *Homesteading: Two Prairie Seasons* (London 1918), pp. 129-30.
23 *Ibid.* From *Toronto Star*, 1 Nov. 1905.
24 *Ibid.* Thompson: Let go after stooking, excursionist G. C. Russell was turned down by three custom threshers before he caught on with a crew. "The Threshers: An Impression," *Canadian Thresherman*, Sept. 1908, pp. 14-15. See also F. M. Cantlon, "The Threshing Crews," *Alberta Historical Review*, autumn 1968.
25 *Ibid.* From Glenbow, CPR, James Colley to C. A. Van Scoy, 7 Feb. 1927, file 711.
26 *Ibid.* From AS, United Farmers of Canada, Saskatchewan Section Papers, "Workmans Compensation," George F. Edwards to Mrs. A. L. Hollis, 5 July 1928.
27 N. S. Federation of Agriculture Report, Micro P.A.N.S., N35, F234, Reel 1-5.
28 Donald MacKay, *The Lumberjacks* (Toronto, 1978), pp. 218-220.
29 Roscoe Fillmore, "One Man's Story," Dalhousie University Archives, MS. 101, pp. 1-9.
30 John Herd Thompson, *op. cit.* Quote is from Kezar interview.
31 *Ibid.* Quote is from Tommy Primrose, "Hired Man Passes from Farm Picture," *Calgary Herald Magazine*, 23 June 1957; interview with Mr. Leon Echenberg, St. Lambert, Quebec, 28 March 1976.
32 Roscoe Fillmore, *op. cit.*, p. 4.
33 D. J. Campbell, *op. cit.*, p. 4.
34 *Ibid.*, pp. 5, 7, 8, 11, 12, 16, 19.
35 Hugh A. Dempsey (ed.) *The Best of Bob Edwards* (Edmonton, 1975), pp. 229, 221.

Footnotes

36 *Ibid.*

Chapter 7
THE 1920S: END OF THE HARVEST TRAINS

1 *Grain Growers Guide*, Winnipeg, July 18, 1923.

2 A. R. McCormack, *Reformers, Rebels and Revolutionaries* (Toronto, 1977), pp. 98-103.

3 Cecelia Danysk, "Farm Workers and Agricultural Development: Changing Conditions of Agricultural Labour in the Prairie West 1900-1930." Paper presented to the CHA Annual Meeting in Guelph, 1984, pp. 17, 19.

4 *Ibid.*

5 *Grain Growers Guide*, September 12, 1923. An English-born IWW organizer in the United States acknowledged the existence of a criminal element in the IWW, although it was never welcomed by the union.

The IWW through its spin-off the AWO (Agricultural Workers' Organization) aimed at organizing farm labourers and harvest hands from the Mexican border to the Canadian prairies. They succeeded in winning better wages, hours and working conditions for workers in the wheat belt. See Patrick Renshaw, *The Wobblies* (New York, 1967), pp. 174-178.

6 Cecelia Danysk, *op. cit.*, p. 16. For Ewen (McEwen) see William Rodney, *Soldiers of the International* (Toronto, 1968), pp. 148, 156n.

7 George V. Haythorne, *op. cit.*, p. 31.

8 *Report of the 60th Annual Trade Union Congress*, Swansea, 1928 (London, 1928), pp. 35, 38.

9 *Winnipeg Free Press*, December 27, 1928.

10 Irving Abella and David Millar, *The Canadian Worker in the Twentieth Century* (Toronto, 1978), pp. 252, 253.

11 Hugh A. Dempsey, *op. cit.*, pp. 135-148, 222, 223.

12 George V. Haythorne, *op. cit.*, p. 39n.

13 *Ibid.*

14 *Ibid.* Also John Herd Thompson, *Bringing in the Sheaves*, pp. 488, 489.

15 The United Farm Women of Manitoba conducted a survey of women's working conditions on the farm in 1922. It revealed that farm women in the West habitually hauled water from an outside well, were expected to do a large amount of manual labour, and lived in relative isolation. Letters printed in *The Grain Growers Guide* (which had some readers in the Maritimes) showed a majority preferring farm life over urban life—better moral tone and pure air—though many bewailed the overwork, monotony, and loneliness of rural life. See Mary Kinnear, "Do you want your daughter to marry a farmer?: Women's Work on the Farm, 1922," Donald H. Akenson (ed.) *Canadian Papers in Rural History* (Gananoque, 1988), pp. 145-154.

16 John Herd Thompson, *op. cit.*, p. 489.

Appendix D
THE INCREDIBLE HARVEST EXCURSION OF 1908 (Cherwinski)

1 Toronto *Daily Star* [hereafter *Star*], 14 August 1908.

2 *Canadian Annual Review*, 1907, 175.

3 See particularly Dept. of the Interior, Immigration Branch [hereaf-

161

ter IB], RG 76, Vol. 131, File 29490, Public Archives of Canada, and the papers of the ministers responsible for labour and agriculture in Manitoba, Saskatchewan, and Alberta.

4 David J. Bercuson, *Fools and Wise Men: The Rise and Fall of the One Big Union* (Toronto 1978), ix-xvi; Donald Avery, *"Dangerous Foreigners": European Immigrant Workers and Labour Radicalism in Canada, 1896-1932* (Toronto 1979), 16-38.

5 IB, Vol. 38, File 839, part 2, O. Smith to W. D. Scott, 1 April 1907.

6 *Ibid.*, Vol. 131, File 29490, part 1, Hugh McKillan to C. Sifton, 20 July 1901.

7 *Ibid.*, Vol. 38, File 839, part 2, Walker to Scott, 8 September 1908; Glenbow-Alberta Institute, Robert G. Trussler Account, AT 873A.

8 IB, Vol. 131, File 29490, part 3, clipping, *Ottawa Free Press*, 12 July 1906.

9 In 1909, for example, W. D. Scott, the Superintendent of Immigration for the Immigration Branch, expressed his concern to his brother Walter, the Premier of Saskatchewan, that the Annual Report of the province's Department of Agriculture was too explicit in the details it presented regarding "...frost, drought, gophers and other enemies to successful crop raising." These looked "very bad in a public document" and were therefore harmful to immigration work. In reply Walter agreed. Sask. Archives Board [hereafter SAB], Motherwell Papers, W. D. Scott to Walter Scott, 29 January 1909, 9824; Scott to Scott, 3 February 1909, 9823.

10 John Herd Thompson, "Bringing in the Sheaves: The Harvest Excursionists, 1890-1929," *Canadian Historical Review* (1978), 467-89; Don D. Lescohier, "Sources of Supply and Conditions of Employment of Harvest Labour in the Wheat Belt," U. S. Dept. of Agriculture Bulletin No. 1211, 22.

11 Saskatchewan, Dept. of Agriculture, *Report* [hereafter SDA Report], 1906, 13-4.

12 *Daily Gleaner* (Fredericton), [hereafter *Gleaner*], 4 August 1908.

13 SDA Report, 1906, 13-14; SAB, Motherwell Papers, Commissioner of Agriculture to Alex Skene, 20 March 1907, 5933; IB, Vol. 131, File 29490, part 1, Robert Kerr to Smart, 11 July 1902; *Star*, 21 August 1908.

14 Thompson, "Bringing in the Sheaves," 469.

15 SDA Report, 1907. 110; IB, Vol. 38, File 839, part 2, Walker to Scott, 8 September 1908.

16 SDA Report, 1907, 107, 110; S. H. Holbrook, *Machines of Plenty* (N. Y. 1955), 123; M. Denison, *Harvest Triumphant* (London 1949), 182.

17 SDA Report, 1907, 107.

18 IB, Vol. 38, File 839, part 2, W. S. Herron to Alta. Dept. of Agriculture, 6 November 1907; clipping from *Montreal Herald*, 21 August 1907; see SAB, Motherwell Papers, 5942-47 for letters and telegrams concerning the shortage of harvesters in September and October of 1907.

19 SDA Report, 1907, 109; (Regina) *Morning Leader* [hereafter *Leader*], 1 August 1908; *Halifax Herald* [hereafter *Herald*], 24 July 1908; Toronto *Globe*, 29 August, 11 September 1908. See also the *Canadian Annual Review* for the variety of estimates made the year before.

20 *Moose Jaw Times* [hereafter *Times*], 24 July 1908; IB, Vol. 38, File

Footnotes

839, part 2, clipping from *Manitou Sun*, 9 November 1905.

21 *Times*, 14 July 1908; *Manitoba Free Press* [hereafter *FP*], 5 and 7 August 1908; SDA Report, 1908, 92-3.

22 *Times*, 14, 24 July 1908; *FP*, 1, 7 August 1908.

23 See *Herald*, 24 July 1908 for a statement by CPR Vice-President Whyte. See also 22 July 1908 and *Gleaner*, 21 July 1908.

24 *Globe*, 5 August 1908; *Star*, 11 August 1908; *Herald*, 29 July 1908; *Gleaner*, 30 July 1908.

25 *FP*, 7 August 1908; *Herald*, 21 July 1908; *Leader*, 1 August 1908.

26 *FP*, 7 August 1908; SDA Report, 1908, 93-3; Derek A. White, *Business Cycles in Canada* (Ottawa 1970), 43; *Star*, 14 August 1908.

27 *Gleaner*, 11 August 1908.

28 *Ibid.*, 12 August 1908.

29 *Star*, 12 August 1908.

30 *Gleaner*, 12 August 1908.

31 *Star*, 14 August 1908. See PAC, Shaughnessy Papers, Letterbook 80, Shaughnessy to J. Osborne, 7 April 1903, and Letterbook 81, Shaughnessy to William Mulock, 9 April 1903, concerning the rationale for colonist cars and complaints of bad conditions associated with them.

32 *Star*, 14 August 1908.

33 *Ibid.*, 15 August 1908.

34 *Ibid.*, 14 August 1908.

35 *Ibid.*, 17 August 1908.

36 *FP*, 15 August 1908.

37 *Ibid.*, 14, 18 and 21 August 1908; *Leader*, 18 August 1908; *Star*, 20 August 1908.

38 *FP* and *Gleaner*, 15 August 1908.

39 *FP*, 15 and 21 August 1908.

40 *Ibid.*, 20 and 21 August 1908; *Leader*, 18 August 1908.

41 *FP*, 19 and 20 August 1908; *Times*, 21 August 1908.

42 *Leader* and *FP*, 18 August 1908; *Star*, 17 August 1908.

43 *Star*, 17 August 1908.

44 *Ibid.* All four were tried on 18 August. Cuttle was released because the liquor theft at Chalk River had occurred off CPR property. Another claimed that he had damaged railway property while very drunk so he was assessed a $20 fine plus damages. The others pleaded not guilty to breaking telegraph pole insulators but a railway constable identified them as sober at the time so they received nine-month terms in Central Prison in Toronto. *FP*, 19 August 1908.

45 *FP*, 18 August 1908.

46 *Ibid.*, 24 August 1908.

47 *Star*, 15 August 1908.

48 *Globe*, 19 August 1908.

49 *Gleaner*, 14 August 1908.

50 *FP*, 15 August 1908.

51 *Ibid.*, 22 August 1908.

52 *Times*, 21 August 1908; *Star*, 22 August 1908.

53 *Times*, 1 September 1908; *FP*, 26 August 1908.

54 *FP*, 15 August 1908.

55 *Ibid.*, 15, 17, 18 August 1908.

56 *Ibid.*, 18 August 1908.

57 *Globe*, 24 August 1908.

58 *FP*, 19 August 1908.

59 *Gleaner*, 21 August 1908.

60 *FP*, 17, 22, 26 August 1908.

61 *Leader*, 24 August 1908.

62 *Globe*, 1 September 1908; IB, Vol. 38, File 839, part 2, Walker to Scott, 8 September 1908.

63 *Leader*, 24, 27, 28 August 1908; *Globe*, 1 September 1908.

64 *Times*, 18 August 1908; *Globe*, 26 August 1908.

65 *Leader*, 19 August 1908.

66 *FP*, 22, 25 August 1908; *Globe*, 24 August 1908; *Times*, 21 August 1908.

67 *Times*, 4, 8 September 1908.

68 *Ibid.*, 28 August 1908; *Globe*, 31 August 1908.

69 *Times*, 25, 28 August 1908.

70 *Ibid.*, 28 August 1908.

71 *Ibid.*, 1 September 1908; *Leader*, 27 August 1908.

72 *Leader*, 27 August 1908.

73 *Ibid.*, 25 August 1908.

74 *Ibid.*; *Globe*, 26 August 1908; *Herald*, 26 August 1908.

75 *Leader*, 26 August 1908.

76 *Ibid.*, 1 September 1908; *Times*, 1 September 1908; *Gleaner*, 28 August 1908; *Globe*, 1, 4 September 1908.

77 *Leader*, 25, 31 August 1908.

78 IB, Vol. 38, File 839, part 2, Walker to Scott, 8 September 1908; SDA Report, 1908, 92-3. See also this report for the detailed distribution of the 14,034 harvesters who found work in the province.

79 SDA Report, 1909, 82.

80 *Ibid.*, 1912, 20-21. This figure differs markedly from Thompson's total of 26,500 but there appears to be no reason to doubt the SDA tally.

81 IB, Vol. 38, File 839, part 2, Walker to Scott, 8 September 1908.

82 SDA Report, 1915, 20-21; SAB, Motherwell Papers, Motherwell to P. J. Phin, 18 July 1913, 5980-3.

83 SDA Report, 1905, 7.

84 *Leader*, 27 August 1908.

85 *Times*, 28 August 1908; *Globe*, 31 August 1908; *Leader*, 26 August 1909. A thousand men unexpectedly joined the 1908 harvest from Winnipeg alone. IB, Vol. 38, File 839, part 2, Walker to Scott, 8 September 1908.

86 *Leader*, 26 August 1909; *Times*, 28 August 1909.

87 *Leader*, 27 August 1908.

Voices from
the Harvest Excursions
FROM INTERVIEWS AND LETTERS

Arbuckle, Wesley MERIGOMISH, NS
Atchison, Jim PUGWASH, NS
Banks, Arthur SHEFFIELD, NB
Beaton, Angus MABOU, NS
Belyea, Abner FREDERICTON, NB
Bigelow, Ralph KINGSPORT, NS
Campbell, Bill NEW GLASGOW, NS
Campbell, John Martin JUDIQUE, NS
Campbell, John Neil SYDNEY MINES, NS
Campbell, Peter MacKenzie SYDNEY, NS
Carter, Harding STELLARTON, NS
Cash, Tom IRISH COVE, NS
Chapman, Fred STELLARTON, NS
Chestnutt, Dr. W. O. HARTLAND, NB
Cooke, Roland BRIDGEVILLE, NS
Corbett, Jim DOMINION, NS
Creighton, Dr. Wilfred HALIFAX, NS
Cunningham, Jack NEW GLASGOW, NS
Dickeson, Herb TAXIS RIVER, NB
Dickie, How WATERVILLE, NS
Dobson, Robert SACKVILLE, NB
Douglas, Charlie TRURO, NS
Doyle, Joe INGONISH, NS
Duncan, Preston FREDERICTON, NB
Elliott, Mrs. BARKER'S POINT, NB
Fraser, Bert MACLELLAN'S BROOK, NS
Fraser, Duncan PINCHER CREEK, ALTA
Fraser, Gilbert SUTHERLAND'S RIVER, NS
Gillis, Dan Allan HALIFAX, NS
Godfrey, John JERSEY, CHANNEL ISLANDS,
UNITED KINGDOM
Goodwin, Lee KINGSPORT, NS
Gourlay, Ernie ANTIGONISH, NS
Gowen, Jim HALIFAX, NS
Grant, A. D. G. PICTOU, NS
Hall, Louis TAYMOUTH, NB
Hanes, Robert SUTHERLAND'S RIVER, NS
Hughes, Ira RIVERTON, NS
Jackson, Frank NORTH SYDNEY, NS

Johnston, John R. BROADWAY, NS
Johnston, Parker DURHAM BRIDGE, NB
Leblanc, Stephen POINT ACONI, NS
MacDonald, Allan GLENCOE, NS
MacDonald, Clyde LYONS BROOK, NS
MacDonald, Duncan SUTHERLAND'S
RIVER, NS
MacDonald, Joe BADDECK, NS
MacDonald, Maurice GLACE BAY, NS
MacDonald, Mr. & Mrs. H. M. ANTIGON-
ISH, NS
MacDonald, Vincent J. ANTIGONISH, NS
MacFarlane, Colin ANTIGONISH, NS
MacFarlane, Jack MARGAREE, NS
MacGillivray, Selina ANTIGONISH, NS
MacGregor, Clarence BROOKVILLE, NS
MacInnis, Dan Hugh ANTIGONISH, NS
MacInnis, W. F. LYONS BROOK, NS
MacIsaac, A. B. ANTIGONISH, NS
MacIsaac, Dan J. DUNMORE, NS
MacIvor, Archie BADDECK, NS
MacKay, Alfred BIG HARBOUR, NS
MacKay, Bert NEW GLASGOW, NS
MacKenzie, Cliff THREE BROOKS, NS
MacLeod, Murdock SYDNEY RIVER, NS
MacNeil, Captain Angus GRAND NAR-
ROWS, NS
MacNeil, Donald LOCH KATRINE, NS
MacNeil, Gus NEW WATERFORD, NS
MacNeil, Reg. EGERTON, NS
MacNeil, Steve BIG POND, NS
MacPherson, Alex Sam ANTIGONISH, NS
Mason, Alf TRENTON, NS
Mason, Stanley MERIGOMISH, NS
Matheson, Roland PICTOU, NS
McCallum, Earl LYONS BROOK, NS
McSorley, Edward FREDERICTON, NB
Murray, Jim BLACK POINT, NS
O'Donnell, Al DOAKTOWN, NB

Partington, Jack STELLARTON, NS
Porter, T. W. BLACK POINT, NS
Priest, Herb CENTRAL CARIBOU, NS
Rae, Art DUMFRIES, NB
Reid, Jim CHURCHVILLE, NS
Robson, Lorne RONKONKOMA, NY
Russell, Carl SHEPODY, NB
Rutherford, Mrs. Jane MacKay SASKA-TOON, SASK
Sampson, Murdock DOMINION, NS
Scott, Redford MARYSVILLE, NB
Shaw, Mrs. Elizabeth CALGARY, ALTA

Smith, Horatius SALMON RIVER, NS
Stewart, Sam PINETREE, NS
Sutherland, George BROOKFIELD, NS
Taylor, Everett CALGARY, ALTA
Thompson, Henry R. NEW GLASGOW, NS
Tibbel, Mrs. PICTOU, NS
Tingley, Neil RIVERSIDE, NB
Tuttle, W. W. WALLACE BAY, NS
Walker, Charlie MARYSVILLE, NB
Weaver, Myles BLISSFIELD, NB
Wickwire, Dr. John LIVERPOOL, NS

About the Author

Angus Anthony MacKenzie was born in New Glasgow, Nova Scotia. His education began in a one-room school in Egerton, and continued through New Glasgow High School, St. Francis Xavier University, and Dalhousie University. He worked as a telephone lineman, farmer, factory worker, and woodsman; he taught at Westville and East Pictou Rural High, and at Xavier Junior College, University of New Brunswick, and University of Manitoba. He retired as Associate Professor of History at St. Francis Xavier University, Antigonish.

About the Cover Painting

These Good Old Thrashing Days is by **Jan Gerrit Wyers**. Born July 20, 1888, in The Netherlands, Jan Wyers died July 4, 1973, in Regina, Saskatchewan. He immigrated to Canada in 1916. He was a self-taught folk painter, and started to paint around 1937. He worked as a homesteader and farmer. He painted memories of scenes in Holland and of farming in Saskatchewan, moments in the working day on a prairie farm. Of his work, he said, "Why shouldn't I show people the way it was before all the big machines took over? I want them to remember."

Breton Books

Wreck Cove, Cape Breton
Nova Scotia B0C 1H0

bretonbooks@ns.sympatico.ca

www.capebretonbooks.com

• SEND FOR OUR FREE CATALOGUE •